ON
$\mathcal{O}$*The*ther
HAND

A Story of Courage
and Triumph in
Spite of a Tragic
Accident

ON
The
Other
HAND

A Story of Courage
and Triumph in
Spite of a Tragic
Accident

JESSICA LANE

Contents

Foreword
by
Courtney Defeo

Take a minute, close your eyes, and imagine this girl from your high school that everyone liked. Imagine the popular, bubbly, kind, athletic one that everyone seemed to know. That's my friend Jessica.

I remember watching her one day and thinking, "Everyone likes her, EVEN the older girls!" Let's be honest. Not all popular folks are likable, but Jessica was beyond likable. She was lovable. She was confident—not egotistical. She was genuinely fun and loved life. She drew people in everywhere she went.

Jessica was (and is) my good friend's sister. So, when I was with Cara, I often got to be with Jessica.

I will never forget the shocking phone call from Cara. Through tears and a shaking voice, she shared that Jessica had been in a very bad car accident. Word quickly spread through our high school that Jessica was alive, but likely paralyzed.

I remember holding onto hope and trying to stay positive—like maybe those rumors were wrong. Maybe the doctors were wrong. Maybe her body would heal from the impact, and she would regain feeling in all of her body.

It was a scary time for her entire family. But that lovable Jessica

1

had an army of high schoolers and community friends praying for her to just be okay. And that group spent hours and days visiting her at The Shepherd Center in Atlanta during her long recovery.

I knew I couldn't do anything but just sit from time to time with Cara. As time passed, we all were faced with accepting what we feared - Jessica was a quadriplegic. I remember feeling shocked and wondering how she would go on with her life. It seemed genuinely unfair. I knew a lot of girls (including me) that would have been better suited for a life so inactive. Maybe it's an insensitive joke, but there's lots of truth to that. Jessica was a ball of fire, action, and fun. I remember wondering, "Why God? Why Jessica?"

In the following pages, you will hear Jessica's amazing story from her perspective. You will soon realize that the same Jessica is still inside. The feisty, strong, determined, and brave teenager used the very gifts God gave her to survive and even thrive in her new normal.

You will be moved to tears as she shares about the many setbacks she has encountered during the last three decades of her life. You will also be moved to awe as you learn how God has shown up in this story. Although many of us will not have the same life battle, we all have our own battles. And we can learn from the strength and hope and wisdom that pours out of her.

Her faith is real. Her faith is tested. Her faith is her sure thing in many uncertain days. I am so very honored to call Jessica a friend and so proud of the life she has built—one determined and faithful choice at a time. She is an inspiration to us all.

I believe God crafts us all with a unique wiring that actually equips us to live our lives. He also equips us and creates us to draw others to Him and to live out His love in a very unique way. I pray that this book stirs something deep inside of you (as it has me). Let's not just sigh and leave sad or sorry or just focused on Jessica.

I pray this story awakens in us a knowing that we were built for a purpose. We can live just surviving this one life, or we can live thriving and open to every twist and turn. We can take our very worst moments and use them for a purpose.

As you naturally wonder, "Would I be able to face her same battle with such courage?" I encourage you to get curious about the same God that is in you. The same God that loves you. What could He do with our stories? What could he do if we surrendered it all to Him and let Him work in and through each of our lives?

So, let's dive in together and allow Jessica's story of faith to inspire us, equip us, and ultimately draw us back to the One who made us.

Acknowledgments

This book would not be possible without the help of the two men who gave me CPR at the scene of the accident, the neurosurgeon on call at Eastside Medical, the doctors, nurses, and therapists at Shepherd Center, my mom, my family, friends and personal nurses and caregivers that have cared for me for the past 32 years, and last but not least, Kimberly Overcast, for interpreting my dictation and her help with spiritual content to make the finished book what it is.

CHAPTER ONE

Adversity Happens

My sixteenth year started off perfectly in my eyes. I was young, vibrant, and full of spontaneity. I was a sophomore in high school, and I was a decent student, even though I enjoyed the social aspects more than anything. I was a cheerleader and a dancer, and I ran track. I had lots of friends, and I enjoyed hanging out with them and going to parties like the typical teenager. I got a car for my birthday. I had fifth-row tickets to see my favorite band, U2, and I was going to go to London to cheer in the New Year's Day parade. So many things were going well for me, and I was so excited. I didn't think life could get any better.

I had a stable home life. My parents were divorced, but they both had remarried. I had the pleasure of gaining six brothers and sisters because of their marriages. I lived with my mom, and I was content, happy, and really enjoying life.

Then a drive on a rainy afternoon changed everything in a matter of moments.

It Happened in a Moment

It was the Labor Day weekend in September of 1992. My mother was leaving on a trip to Florida that morning, but something in her knew. Mothers have that deep sense of knowing in the pits of their stomachs when it comes to their children. As my mother prepared to leave, she grabbed hold of me in a tight embrace and didn't want to let go. I even said to her, "Mom, it's all right. I'll be fine. You're just going to Florida for the weekend." She reluctantly let me go and walked out the door.

It was one of those wet, rainy days that can make just about anyone miserable. I was staying with Jill, who was one of my best friends, while my parents were out of town. We were usually inseparable, but on Saturday morning, I decided to stay at her house and take a nap while she went with her family to her sister's softball game. Not long after they left, the phone rang. On a whim, I decided to go get a bite to eat at Hardee's with my friend Trisha. While we were at the restaurant, she and I agreed we needed to go check up on her boyfriend because she was having suspicions about him. He wasn't supposed to be home, but just as we drove past his house, we saw him pulling out of the driveway. Caution went to the wind, and off we went, following after him but staying far enough behind that he couldn't see us.

> *Your moments are precious. Don't waste them.*

That decision changed everything. A drive in the rain with a friend turned into tragedy. We started hydroplaning. I felt the car go out of control, and we crossed the center lane. We hit another car close to head-on, and the impact rattled my whole body. In that moment, time felt as if it were standing still. I remember screaming Trisha's name and then feeling hunched over. I could feel the life beginning to slip out of my body as I started to black out. Could this be it? Was this the end of my life?

Life is full of moments. As humans, we like to feel in control, but the truth is that we don't really know for certain what is going to happen from one moment to the next. Your moments are precious. Don't waste them. Your life can change or even end in the blink of an eye or with the hydroplane of a car. The Bible tells us, "You do not know what will happen tomorrow. For what is your life? It is even a vapor that appears for a little time and then vanishes away" (James 4:14, ESV).

Little did I know at that moment that the seat belt had broken my neck. In an instant, there was nothing. I was lifeless and not breathing; my body turned peaked and blue.

My friend's boyfriend, whom we were supposedly secretly following, saw us get in the wreck because he knew we were following him all along. We were trying to stay hidden and be mysterious, but instead, God made us visible so He could use that young man to save my life. He jumped in the back seat of the car and laid the seat back, being careful not to move my body. He started CPR and brought me back to life. He continued CPR for fifteen minutes, along with another man who later disappeared from the scene and was never identified (I believe he was an angel) until the EMTs arrived. He was a cross-country runner, and even with his strong lungs, he said that fifteen minutes felt like a lifetime.

I was transported by ambulance to Eastside Medical Center. I remember being slightly conscious when I arrived in the emergency room. All I could see were white lights around me and what looked like a woman's face. It resembled those scenes in the movies where you can see from someone else's perspective when he or she wakes up from surgery or something traumatic and can hardly see other people because it's all bright and blurry. I remember them telling me I had been in a car accident, but then I blacked out again.

I had a C2 spinal cord injury, an injury that is often fatal, even more so back then. By the grace of God, there was a neurosurgeon working in the ER that day. He gave me the proper steroid medicine to keep the swelling down in my neck, which lessened the damage to my spinal cord by taking the extra pressure off—a big blessing. But I was paralyzed from the neck down, and I was placed on a ventilator to help me breathe.

When the accident happened, I had no identification on me, so they had no idea who I was. I was, therefore, reported as a Jane Doe. Even though Trisha knew who I was, she was so upset that she kept calling me by the name of the girl I was staying with, Jill Claborn. While I was being transported to the hospital, the police at the scene of the accident contacted the principal of my high school. He met the police and Trisha's boyfriend at the school so they could flip through the yearbook, find my picture, and identify me. Once I was identified, they were able to notify my family.

My mom woke up that morning uneasy and unsure of what was to come. She had a sick feeling in the pit of her stomach all day long. She knew something was wrong, but she had no idea what was happening to me five hundred miles away. Then, the thing she had been fearing all day became a reality. The phone rang, and my brother Heath told her she needed to call the emergency room right away. When she called the ER, the doctor didn't give my mom very many details other than to tell her it was very serious and that she needed to fly home from Florida rather than drive. Terrified, nervous, and unsure about my survival, she and my stepdad left their car in Florida and hopped on the fastest flight they could get to come home. While on the phone with the ER doctor, my mom approved my transfer to Shepherd Spinal Center—now called just Shepherd Center—a spinal cord hospital in Atlanta, and I arrived there just five hours after my accident. They shaved half the hair off my head and placed me in traction in the ICU. I don't remember any of it.

When my mom arrived at Shepherd in a taxi straight from the airport and walked in the main entrance, she saw people she knew everywhere: family, friends, students from my high school, and their parents. She barely had time to take it in because she was immediately brought to see my admitting physician, Dr. Leslie, who explained how bad my injury was and how difficult my life would be. But my mom just wanted to know one thing: "Is she going to live?"

The doctor paused before answering. "I think so."

"Then we will deal with the rest of it one step at a time," my mom responded.

When they took my mom upstairs to see me in the ICU, our pastor, Dr. Gannon, was waiting in the hallway. He grabbed both my mom's hands and assured her, "God will be with her every minute." And He was. And He is. And He will be forever.

Waking Up

Three days later, I became aware of my surroundings again, and I wondered what had happened. How could this have come to pass, and why? Did I do something wrong?

While those were some of my initial thoughts, I don't think I was being punished. While it is true that sometimes the bad things that happen to us are the consequences of our sin, it is also true that sometimes these things just happen. While trying to follow my friend's boyfriend in the rain may not have been the wisest choice, it was not as if the accident was the result of drunk driving or something like that. Tragedy just happens sometimes. The circumstances of life sweep in and everything is changed forever in an instant. A loved one dies, a tragic fire takes your house, or a tornado destroys a town—I don't believe God makes these things happen. It's just the way things happen in a fallen world.

When I woke up in the hospital, my dad was the first person I saw, at least that I can remember. I didn't even realize I was paralyzed. I asked him where I was, and he explained to me again that I had been in a car accident. All I wanted to know was if I would be better in time to go to the U2 concert and London. My dad's response was, "Well, we'll see."

I had no idea what a long, hard journey I was facing would be, but I was still so afraid. I don't really remember the moment when I first found out I was paralyzed. And truthfully, in those first few days, it didn't dawn on me that they meant forever. I really didn't think anything. I do remember crying, but even the tears didn't last long. I just kind of felt a little numb and unsure of what was to come.

I had surgery a few days later to have a tracheotomy tube put in, and I remained in ICU for two more weeks in traction. To be able to start rehab and to keep my neck stable and still, they placed me in a halo traction device—a cervical brace used to immobilize cervical fractures and aid in the healing of spinal injuries while still allowing someone to be mobile. It consists of a metal ring, or halo, attached to the skull with screws, and a lined vest that is worn on the torso and attached to the halo with rods. The day they put it on, I had to lie there while they put metal screws into my skull, only giving me a little numbing medicine. I can still hear the sound of those screws today. I couldn't feel any pain, but I had a sensation of them, and I was aware of the intensity of what was going on. It was very uncomfortable, and eventually, one of the screws on the vest dug into the back of my shoulder, causing a deep wound called a pressure sore. I still have a horrible scar from it today.

With the halo in place, I was finally able to get out of bed. The first time they ever put me in a chair, I cried. It seemed so out of place and foreign. You can't move anything, you can't breathe on your own, and you've been lying down for weeks, unconscious half the time. Then you're thrust into an uncomfortable chair that doesn't even fit your body and are told to get used to it. I remember thinking, "Is this really happening?"

Needless to say, learning how to tolerate sitting in a chair for any length of time while in a strange environment was sometimes overwhelming. The halo made it even more unbearable, and I was supposed to wear it for two long months. I dreaded every day of those two months, but about six weeks later, on Halloween, something happened. My mom decided to dress me up for Halloween as a bird in a cage. As if having a halo with pins screwed into your skull wasn't conspicuous enough, she used the halo as a prop for my Halloween costume. Gee, thanks, Mom—that wasn't embarrassing at all.

That night, when I was getting into bed, I felt one of the pins on my halo scrape down my forehead, and blood started dripping down my face. I screamed to my mother and the nurse that my halo was slipping. At first, they said that was impossible, but then they looked and realized that it was true. One of the pins had worked its way out of my skull, and they had to hold it back to keep it from going in my eye. They paged the doctor, who left a Halloween party and ended up taking my halo off early.

Taking Off the Mask

When I look back at when I had the halo removed, I see it as the time when I took off my Halloween costume for good. The early removal of my halo was a nice, although slightly scary, surprise, and I haven't missed the halo (or the Halloween costume) one bit.

> *Don't allow fear to make you believe*
> *that you need to hide behind a mask.*

My halo made me feel bound. It made me feel as if people couldn't see the real me because my head was surrounded by a glaring reminder of my condition. It was a mask, hiding who I really am. And getting rid of it was liberating.

There are times in life when you need to get rid of the costume and get rid of the mask that is hiding who you really are or keeping you chained to the past. Don't allow fear to make you believe that you need to hide behind a mask because of what other people might think if they saw the real you. Fear keeps you in prison. Fear keeps you chained. Just like I got rid of my halo, get rid of the things that make you feel bound to the past. Don't carry them around like so much excess baggage. Don't wear them as shackles around your wrists, your ankles, and your neck— because let's face it: chains don't look good on you, or anyone else for that matter.

Take a Deep Breath

With the halo gone and my neck more stable, it was crunch time. At Shepherd, they make you work and learn. You have occupational therapy and physical therapy every day except on the weekends. The therapists taught me key things, such as how to drive my chair, how to use a computer, and how to sign things using a pen in my mouth.

The nurses also put me to work. They taught me how to pay attention to and maintain control of my body and my environment, even though I couldn't move. I learned how to pay attention to details with my body to make sure things were right. I learned about everything from skincare to dressing properly to maintaining my general health. They taught me everything they could so I could live as independently as possible despite my injury.

I had to take classes on my body and how and why it functions the way it does after my injury. I learned all about the spinal cord and how it works. I learned how and why certain things happen differently after an injury like mine and how to deal with it. I even had to take classes about how to be intimate after a spinal cord injury. (That was an awkward class at the age of sixteen, but I'm grateful for the information.)

Although the rehab and classes felt hard, they were honestly the easy part. I was still very sick and unstable, and there were many bumps in the road along the way. The slightest wrong move caused me to have a vagal nerve response, and I would go into cardiac arrest. The alarm would sound all over the hospital, and doctors, nurses, and the respiratory therapist would come running to give me CPR. It occurred three times over the course of my six-month stay at Shepherd. Every time that happened, I ended up back in ICU for a time, and rehab stopped until I recovered. It was awful.

Yet God took one of those awful times and turned it into good, just like it says in Romans 8:28, "And we know that for those who love God, all things work together for good, for those who are called according to his purpose."

My mom and a nurse were transferring me from my chair to the bed, and yet again, I coded. As they got the crash cart and shoved my mom out of the way, she hit her knees, praying at my bedside. At that moment, because she did not know what else to do, she totally let God be in control. She cried out to Him, saying, "Lord, if You want her, then You can have her back. I only ask that if You let her live, please send her back better because she has worked so hard up to this point."

As I was being transported back to the ICU, my doctor was running alongside the gurney, using a manual resuscitator to give me air. All of a sudden, the tube accidentally popped off my trach, and at that moment, he thought he saw me trying to take a breath on my own. In a moment, I went from being vent-dependent for the rest of my life to having the hope of actually being able to breathe on my own.

To test if my diaphragm was actually working, they placed me in a machine that could see if my diaphragm was moving when I tried to take a breath. They removed me from the ventilator and told me to try to breathe on my own. I remember thinking, "Are you kidding me?" I gasped in what I imagined felt like a breath (but what really felt like suffocation), and lo and behold, my diaphragm moved.

A few days later, I was lying on a mat in the gym for physical therapy, and a respiratory therapist I was very close to came in and said, "Well, your diaphragm works. You want to try it?" With fear and trepidation, I reluctantly agreed. She took me off the ventilator, and I lay there and breathed on my own for ten minutes. It felt like an eternity, and I thought I was suffocating the whole time. I wasn't; it just felt that way. The respiratory therapist carefully monitored me and made sure my blood oxygen level was good the whole time. Normally, when you breathe, you don't think about it. It just comes naturally as an involuntary response. But when you're being weaned off the ventilator, you have to teach yourself how to breathe again. Every breath needs a thought, and you feel as if you're gasping for air. I used to beg them to put me back on, but somewhere deep inside, I didn't want them to. I had to find the will and determination within me to keep moving forward and to keep pressing on.

Life is like that sometimes. You may feel as if you are suffocating, but you need to press on. Don't give up. Staying on the ventilator would have been the easier choice in many respects; Breathing would not have required any effort on my part. But easy isn't always best. In fact, I would say easy isn't best for a large portion of the time. Challenges and obstacles, when faced, make you stronger. They build you up. They prepare you to conquer even tougher challenges—and trust me, there are always tougher challenges ahead. So, during those times you feel as if you are suffocating; take a deep breath and press on. You can do it!

"But one thing I do: forgetting what lies behind and straining forward to what lies ahead, I press on toward the goal for the prize of the upward call of God in Christ Jesus" (Philippians 3:13–14).

I kept pressing on. Every day, they took me off the ventilator, and each time, I was off it for a longer period of time. Ten minutes became thirty minutes; thirty minutes became an hour. An hour became two hours, then three, then four, and so on. It took two months, but the day finally came when I no longer needed the ventilator. We even had a funeral ceremony for the vent, celebrating my no longer needing it. While it was exciting, it was still scary. I actually used to watch my chest to make sure it was moving up and down.

After I was able to breathe on my own, they decided to try and get rid of my trach as well. They

> *Easy isn't always best.*

placed a special device in my trach hole to keep the hole open while closing the airway at the same time so I could breathe through my nose. I was so excited to be able to talk audibly again. I called my mom on the phone and said, "Mom, listen, I can talk out loud." She was so excited to hear my voice again. Unfortunately, before my mom even got back to the hospital, we discovered that night that my chest muscles weren't strong enough to cough up phlegm, and I choked and coded again. When they went to put my trach back in, they discovered the device had accidentally moved out of my trach hole, and the hole had already closed up in those few short hours. With no time to do anything else, they had to trach me again right there at the bedside. The incident scared me badly, and to this day, I have never tried to remove my trach again.

Free at Last

Beginning to understand a new way of living was often quite scary. While there were so many things I was afraid of medically because of my unstable condition, there was also this huge fear of the unknown—about what it would be like to live as a quadriplegic out in the real world, beyond the safety of the hospital. It was one thing to become somewhat comfortable within the confines of the hospital, but I wondered if I could actually go outside among other people and feel comfortable. It was an overwhelming thought.

My first outing was to the Coca-Cola Museum in downtown Atlanta. Shepherd piled a group of us into a van equipped to carry several chairs, and off we went. Every bump in the road felt like a knife in my back. Finally, we arrived. We all rolled out of the van and into the museum. I felt as if everyone were staring at me like I was an alien from another planet. It was very awkward and weird. Although it was scary and unnerving, there was also some freedom in it. Actually being able to go out of the hospital and be out in the real world again was fun. It gave me hope for what was to come next.

My first visit home was a test run over Thanksgiving

God intended for you to walk in freedom.

weekend. I was so scared of being out of the hospital and on my own with just my family. I was anxious that something would happen without the comfort and protection of the doctors and nurses around. The only thing I remember about that time was the fear. The trip back to the hospital could not come quickly enough for me. Yet, while the hospital felt safe, it was no place to live forever.

Because here's the deal: God intended for you to walk in freedom. He intended you to live an abundant life. And He paid a high price so you could do so.

"For freedom, Christ has set us free" (Galatians 5:1).

"I came that they may have life and have it abundantly" (John 10:10).

The problem is that we tend to get stuck in places that we hate or aren't good for us or aren't part of God's plan for our lives just because they are familiar and, in that sense, comfortable. We stay in prison because it is what we are used to. And the enemy of our souls likes nothing better than to keep us chained to the past. The first part of the abundant life verse just quoted says, "The thief comes only to steal and kill and destroy." Satan wants to steal your joy, kill your hope, and destroy your faith. He wants you to stay shackled so you don't fulfill your God-given purpose. He doesn't want you to be free. He wants you bound.

But as a son or daughter of the Lord Most High, you are free. The Word promises, "If the Son sets you free, you will be free indeed." If you have accepted the abundant grace and mercy of the Lord Jesus Christ, if you have trusted Him to be your Savior, you are free. You are free indeed. But you need to choose to walk in that freedom.

The Book of Isaiah paints an interesting picture of a prisoner, "Awake, awake! Put on your strength.... Shake yourself from the dust, arise.... Loose yourself from the bonds of your neck, O captive daughter of Zion" (Isaiah 52:1-2, NKJV)!

It is the image of a woman who is still sitting in prison, even though, in reality, she is free. She has become accustomed to her bondage, to the chains, to the dirt and dust of her prison cell. She has the strength and the ability to walk in freedom, but her complacency has caused her not to use that strength and even to fall asleep when the chance for freedom has presented itself. The Lord has unlocked her shackles and opened the prison door, but she is still living in prison even though she is free—all she needs to do is wake up, remove the unlocked shackles that have been keeping her bound, shake the dust and dirt of her past off, and walk out the prison door into an abundant life of freedom.

Perhaps you are like that woman. Perhaps you are sitting in a dark, damp, dirty prison cell with chains around your wrists, your ankles, and your neck. They may be chains of the past, of fear, of sin, of addiction, of hopelessness, or countless other things. And you continue to stay in that prison because it is familiar. But the time has come for you to wake up! Jesus unlocked your chains, whatever they may be when He died on the cross. His last three words, "It is finished!" (John 19:30), were a proclamation of truth. The work of setting you free has been completed. It is done. There is nothing left to be done on His part. But you need to choose to walk out your freedom. So, wake up! Take those chains off! Loose yourself! Shake off the dust, and walk out that prison door that Jesus flung open wide just for you.

When the apostle Paul declared that it was for freedom, Christ set us free; He also said this, "Stand firm, therefore, and do not submit again to a yoke of slavery" (Galatians 5:1).

You are free. So, stand in freedom. Walk in it. Share the joy of that freedom with others. Don't let the enemy of your soul steal, kill, or destroy anything that God has for you. Say goodbye to your past, to the things holding you back from your purpose. If need be, have a funeral for the things that are keeping you bound, the way we did for my ventilator. Shake off those chains. Because just like the hospital was no place for me to live forever, your prison—whatever it may be—is no place for you to live forever. You have been called to abundant life.

During my time in the hospital, I gradually became more stable, and my therapy and all my training came to an end. I spent six long months at Shepherd Spinal Center. I must say, those six months were quite interesting. The whole hospital became like family, and I learned all the juicy secrets about everyone—who was dating whom, who wanted to be dating whom, and all kinds of stuff. And while it began to feel like home, it wasn't home. The time to get back out into the real world had finally come. On March 5, 1993, exactly six months to the day from when I arrived, I was discharged from the hospital.

CHAPTER TWO

Stretching Out

Waking up that first morning after I left the hospital felt surreal. I was in my room in my house, but it felt like a whole new place. We lived in a three-story house. My room was in the basement, so some adaptations had to be made to the house and property. Bill, my stepdad, built ramps around the backyard so I could get into the basement from the driveway. He also built a ramp in the garage so I could get into the kitchen on the second level. The shower in the basement bathroom was also adapted so I could lie on a special stretcher and get a bath.

I knew all the adjustments were necessary, but the homey feeling I once had disappeared in the midst of it all. My old four-poster bed was replaced by a hospital bed. Medical equipment and supplies sat out where anyone and everyone could see them. The changes left my home looking sterile—more like a hospital than a home—and the whole atmosphere made me feel sick as if there were something incredibly wrong with me. The combination of facing my new reality and all the changes it brought left me feeling depressed. All I wanted to do was just sit there and stare at the wall. Family and friends would try to engage me in conversations or do goofy things to get me to laugh, and I would just sit there, staring.

Sometimes, I wandered outside and tried to enjoy the beautiful weather, but I stayed relatively quiet and withdrawn. I guess I was just trying to soak everything in. I was already feeling overwhelmed, but then, just about a week after I came home from the hospital, the beautiful weather turned into a blizzard, which became known as the "Storm of the Century," and dropped anywhere from four to sixteen inches of snow across the Atlanta area. Temperatures plummeted, all the roads shut down, and the power went out all over the city.

The whole house was getting really cold with the power off. There was a gas fireplace upstairs in the living room, but I wasn't quite sure how I was going to get up there. As a quadriplegic, I certainly couldn't roll out into the deep snow and drive my chair to the upstairs through the yard as usual, and electric wheelchairs are way too heavy to be carried anywhere. But Bill picked me up out of my wheelchair, carefully carried my dead weight upstairs, and placed me in a papasan chair with a footstool by the fireplace. It was not the most comfortable of chairs, but it worked for the occasion. I was bundled from head to toe with multiple layers, along with a hat and gloves, and we hung sheets in all the doorways to keep the heat in the room.

My Uncle Sidney, because he was a DeKalb County police officer at the time, was able to get his hands on a small generator from Georgia Power. With chains on the tires of his patrol car, he brought it over to us in case we needed to have power for the medical equipment I had to use. As the storm continued, we passed the time by playing games, reading books, and telling stories. When night came, I couldn't stay in the same position in the papasan chair all night, so Bill dragged my mattress upstairs and laid it on the floor for me to sleep on. It was a long, scary night. The next morning, even though the storm wasn't over, the power came back on so I could return to my wheelchair and the comforts of my room downstairs. It was definitely a learning experience. When you first get home from the hospital, you don't even think about the kind of provisions you need every day, let alone what you will need in an emergency.

The storm was a nerve-racking beginning to my new adventures at home, but I was also still very unstable. I don't know if it was just the way my neck healed after the break or if it was the anatomy of my body, but regular tracheotomy tubes wouldn't fit in my trachea. They would cut off my airway with the slightest wrong move, and I was also allergic to the material they were made of, causing scar tissue to form around my trach. I had surgery seven times to have the scar tissue removed from my trachea because it caused me to have difficulty breathing. Finally, a surgeon figured out I needed an extra-long, less curved tracheotomy tube made of silicone. Once the tracheotomy tube was below the injury level and made of a different material, I finally began to heal. Although I was glad to have that behind me, every medical procedure that occurred left me more and more scared, and my imagination would sometimes get the best of me.

Driving Out the Fear

With everything being so fresh and new, I was still a little apprehensive about being away from the hospital, as well as about the many things causing me to be unstable. At first, I let that apprehension get the best of me at times. Rather than controlling it, I let it control me. I lay awake at night, anxiously watching myself breathe. I counted how many times my heart beat in a minute to make sure I was actually still alive. Not only was I physically paralyzed, I was allowing fear to paralyze me emotionally. Circumstances can sometimes cause fear to set in and encompass your whole life. But "God has not given us a spirit of fear, but of power and of love and of a sound mind" (2 Tim. 1:7, NKJV). That last part—a sound mind—is especially important when anxious thoughts are consuming you.

The truth is that Satan wants you to be paralyzed physically, emotionally, and spiritually. He wants to steal, kill, and destroy both you and the purpose God has for your life. One of the best ways for him to accomplish that is by filling your mind with anxious thoughts, worries, and, above, all fear. But God has given you a sound mind. He has given you the tools you need to drive out the fear, to replace the lies of the enemy with the truth.

The Bible talks about "casting down arguments and every high thing that exalts itself against the knowledge of God, bringing every thought into captivity to the obedience of Christ" (2 Cor. 10:5). When the enemy shoots his fiery arrows of fear and lies at you, you need to raise up your shield of faith and counteract every false thought he sends your way. And it is not just a matter of thinking, "I am not going to think that," or, "I am not going to buy into that lie." You need to bring every thought into captivity to the obedience of Christ by replacing it with the truth.

So when the enemy tries to make you worry, get rid of the worry by replacing it with truth: "Look at the birds of the air: they neither sow nor reap nor gather into barns, and yet your heavenly Father feeds them. [Am I] not of more value than they?" (Matt. 6:26).

When the enemy tries to make you afraid, kick the fear to the curb by replacing it with truth: "God has not given [me] a spirit of fear, but of power and of love and of a sound mind" (2 Tim. 1:7,

NKJV).

"I sought the LORD, and he answered me and delivered me from all my fears" (Ps. 34:4).

"The LORD is my light and my salvation; whom shall I fear? The LORD is the stronghold of my life; of whom shall I be afraid?" (Ps. 27:1).

Whatever tactics the enemy uses to attack you, find promises from the Word of God to counterattack. Jesus Himself set the example for us by doing that very thing when Satan tempted Him in the wilderness. Everything Satan tried to use against Him was countered by truth from the Word. (See Matthew 4:1-11.)

Before my accident, I was active and outgoing. Fear was not in my vocabulary. I would seek out ways to pump that adrenaline. I bungee jumped, rode on the scariest of roller coasters, and made plans with my uncle to go skydiving one day. But I became imprisoned by fear because of my circumstances. I needed to figure out a way to recapture the fearless energy I once had to help me with everything that happened. For weeks, fear kept me from trying new things or moving forward in ways that could open up different opportunities for me.

One of the first things I learned at Shepherd was how to drive my power chair, and while I wanted the independence of driving myself around on my own, fear told me I couldn't have it. For a few weeks, I refused to drive myself around in my chair. Getting pushed around felt safer and less frightening. It was kind of like that imprisoned woman in Isaiah 52 I talked about. I actually had the freedom and ability to drive my chair on my own, but getting pushed around was familiar and, therefore, more comfortable, so I didn't take advantage of the freedom I had.

Then, one day, shortly after I got out of the hospital, my mom, Bill, and I went to a big antique warehouse. Because I refused to drive myself, Bill pushed me around the warehouse everywhere. I kept asking him to take me here or there, but he never would; he just took me places he wanted to go. Finally, after going to see things I didn't want to see and missing out on everything that I wanted to see, I got really frustrated. That day, I finally got bold enough to realize that living in fear wasn't working. If I wanted different results, I was going to have to make some changes. It was the first small step toward conquering my fear and getting some independence back.

I learned how to drive my chair myself at Shepherd, but actually doing it out in the world scared me. To drive my chair independently, I use what they call a sip-and-puff control device. To drive forward, I puff hard against a straw, and the chair moves forward. To stop, I sip in. To move backward, I sip hard on the straw and puff on it to stop. To turn right, I puff softly on the straw, and to turn left, I sip softly on the straw. Then it's just a combination of sips and puffs, kind of like a code. It was perhaps not the best thing to still be practicing in an antique shop, but I was determined I was going to go see what I wanted to see. It was such a monumental moment that I remember it like it was yesterday.

That day taught me a few things: Although I couldn't move, God still made a way for me to be independent, even in a small way. If you want a different outcome, then you have to seize the opportunities God gives you. And attitude, attitude, attitude is everything! I could have sat there, cried, and pouted, "Oh poor me, I can't walk. I might as well just sink into a depression. After all, I'm paralyzed, so he should be catering to where I want to go." If I had done that, I would still be sitting in a corner by myself today or going places I don't want to go. I would still be sitting in a prison even though the door had been unlocked and flung open. I would be missing out on that sweet, small bit of independence God gave me—the ability to drive my chair myself. Since I have to depend on others for so many things, why in the world would I choose to just go places I don't want just to go because I don't want to put in the effort to try something different? Was it scary? Yes. Did I run into things? Absolutely (but thankfully, no antiques). Because I wanted a different result, I kept practicing and practicing, over and over, until I did feel comfortable. Now, I drive myself all over the place.

I received another sweet touch of independence when I learned how to use a computer. I use a head-mounted laser system that consists of a device on top of my head and another device on top of my computer screen. The two devices communicate with a laser that controls the mouse as I move my head. A straw is attached to the headset, and I blow into it to give a command, just like someone able-bodied clicks on the mouse. There is a keyboard on the screen, and I point and select each letter to type. This opened up a whole world of opportunity. I could email people all by myself, do my own homework, make a graphics project, read a book and flip my own pages, and even work on this book. I could have private conversations on instant messenger, explore the internet, and all kinds of other things. They have even adapted video games so I can use them. I am so thankful because it makes the whole process a lot easier.

Those first few weeks were the beginning of my recovery from the stronghold of fear that grabbed hold of my life because of my circumstances. As I continued to move ahead slowly but surely, the fear began to dissipate, and strength began to rise. An accident such as mine can not only disable you physically, but if you allow it,

> *If you want a different outcome, then you have to seize the opportunities God gives you.*

it can also disable you from living life. And the truth is that anything that keeps you bound in fear can be disabling.

Jesus said, "I came that they may have life and have it abundantly" (John 10:10). You are meant to be living an abundant life, full of love, faith, hope, joy, and purpose. Don't let fear get in the way. Don't let fear keep you in prison. Don't let fear keep you bound in shackles you were never meant to wear. Stand fast in your liberty (Gal. 5:1). Don't let the lies of the enemy keep you from abundant life.

I was not going to let fear control me. It was time for me to get back to the land of the living, scared or not. While I would have loved to just stay home and hide in my room, I knew I had to get back to living life. And among other things, that meant going back to school. Gwinnett County Public Schools, and Parkview High School in particular, went out of their way to make sure my school was accessible and even provided a caregiver to go to school with me. With all the preparations in place, the day finally came when I rolled into my high school for the first time. I felt awkward and strange, and it seemed as if everyone was staring at me as I rolled down the hall. It took some time, but eventually, I got used to my new way of getting around. Classes and social events continued as they always had. I met friends in the hall between classes, and we found places around the campus courtyard to get together for lunch. I went to parties, the movies, and the Friday night football games. Life carried on.

> *You are meant to be living an abundant life, full of love, faith, hope, joy, and purpose. Don't let fear get in the way.*

Moving Forward

Even though I settled into the new way of doing things, there were still some hard times. I missed dance, cheerleading, and track. Sometimes, I caught myself sitting on the sidelines, remembering what used to be. I wondered why this happened to me and if I would ever be able to run and dance freely as I once had. But I quickly realized that I couldn't focus on the whys or what ifs—I had to focus on what was and what could be.

When you face a situation like mine, looking back or looking too far ahead can leave you depressed and sad. It can imprison your mind with racing thoughts about all kinds of scenarios, however improbable. I had to start taking my thoughts captive. All I needed to think about was what I could do day by day. So, I shifted my focus to my schoolwork and my friends. With a lot of hard work, I was able to make up for the six months of school I missed while I was in the hospital and graduate with my class. In May 1995, all 450 of my classmates gathered on the stadium football field and prepared to walk or roll, in my case, to get our diplomas. As my name was called and I came across the field to get my diploma, everyone in the stadium was on their feet in a standing ovation. But the moment didn't feel real. Thoughts of what I was going to do next ran across my mind. High school had become another safe haven, but now what was I going to do? Before my accident, my plan had been to go to Auburn University and eventually law school. That was no longer a desire, but I had no idea what was next.

After thinking long and hard, I decided to take it slow and begin college locally. I applied for and received a special scholarship, so I began taking classes. I came a few classes short of getting an associate degree in journalism, but I ended up not finishing because of some medical complications. While I desired a career of some kind, I knew going to college someplace was too difficult at the time because of some things going on with me medically. I decided to take a break and get physically stronger.

A few years later, I discovered a love for design, took a home-based correspondence course in interior design, and was certified to work as a professional interior designer. I tried some different things, but I had a strong desire to continue serving others. I wanted to be able to encourage people in their faith and be able to advise them from a scriptural perspective. So, I decided to get certified in Christian counseling to learn how to speak to people better and encourage them in different ways. I did a home-based study through the Center for Biblical Counseling and was certified as a Christian counselor. I have used the information I learned from that course many times since then to help me advise others. While I have never desired to sit in an office and counsel people in a formal setting, I appreciate how the knowledge I gained helps me talk to people when opportunities present themselves.

Life then took me to a season when all I really did was enjoy life and serve the Lord with no particular agenda. During that time, a friend at church was pursuing a music career. Through speaking to him, I discovered a love for music I had not realized I had. I then took some online courses to be certified in the music business. All my schooling helped me grow and develop into the person I am today. With each passing year, different opportunities presented themselves, and while I don't use any of my studies to have a specific career right now, I use my different skills all time. From decorating my own house or helping friends decorate their own houses to speaking encouraging words to a friend or even a stranger—the things I learned and the skills I developed all remain a part of my life.

My living situation also provided opportunities to grow and stretch. My childhood home was clearly not a good fit since it was three stories. For a while I lived in a ranch house with my mother, my stepdad, and my grandmother. It was wonderful to finally be in an accessible house, where I could go to the kitchen without having to go out to the backyard, up the ramp, and through the garage. However, four adults living in such close quarters was too much for all of us. We were living on top of each other and constantly arguing.

But then, one day, we saw a for-sale sign on some property just around the corner. It was a thirteen-acre farm with a ranch house and two garage apartments, one upstairs and one downstairs. It needed a lot of work, but my designer's eye could see the potential. I bought it, and we began fixing it up. I lived in the house while my mother and Bill lived in the apartment upstairs and my grandmother lived in the apartment downstairs. Having our own spaces was great. And when the property next door went up for sale about a year later, my mother and Bill moved there. They were about a football field away, which was close enough to help if I needed them but far enough away to give us all plenty of breathing room.

Having my own house to fix up was exciting. I quickly learned that it didn't have to be all sterile and hospital-like for it to be functional for my life as a quadriplegic. If you walked into my house to-

> *You have already passed by your past, so leave it behind. It's time to move forward.*

day, you wouldn't know someone disabled lived here. All medical equipment and supplies are tucked away, and everything looks like it would be in a typical home. I can still use regular furniture and sleep in a regular bed. I have a four-poster queen-sized bed with a regular mattress. It works for me even better and is more comfortable than the hospital bed. Having my home look normal was important to me because it helped me feel like myself instead of a stranger in my own home. I didn't need a constant reminder everywhere I looked of my injury. I felt that I couldn't grow, learn, and adapt to my new way of life if I felt as if I were in the hospital at home. I think it is that way for a lot of us. Sometimes, it is hard to move forward when we are constantly reminded of the past.

God promised that "if anyone is in Christ, he is a new creation; old things have passed away; behold, all things have become new" (2 Cor. 5:17, NKJV). If the enemy is trying to keep you stuck in the past or make you feel condemned, it may be time to get rid of the things that remind you of who you once were before you became a new creation in Christ. Here is the truth: God promised that *all things* have become new. You have already passed by your past, so leave it behind. It's time to move forward. Don't carry reminders of the old you around like baggage or, worse, like chains. God has made you new. Get rid of the things that might make you think otherwise, and move forward.

My home has become my haven. I have no idea what God has planned or how long I'll live here, but I am happy and privileged to have a place that feels like home. Having the stability of a good home and family support around you is extremely helpful when you face challenges and obstacles, and I thank God that I have those things. The stretching and adapting that I needed to do in the first few years after my accident were just the beginning of my road to recovery. While I have made great strides and changes over the years, recovery in all areas takes time. When you are paralyzed, your whole world changes physically, mentally, and emotionally. I knew I wanted to still live and live life to the fullest, but where could I find the strength, determination, and desire to keep on living when things sometimes seemed so dark and hopeless?

CHAPTER THREE

Emotions Run Deep

Picture yourself chained and bound. You can't move your legs. You can't move your arms. You can't move anything other than your head. Then, silence your voice to a complete whisper, which cannot be heard unless someone is right next to you. That is what it is like for me. That is the world I live in.

Sometimes, when I'm all alone and unable to get to anyone, I feel as if I've been buried alive. It's just psychological, and it seems silly, but it can feel real. Living life paralyzed and unable to speak audibly definitely took an adjustment period. Every day, I have to depend on other people to get things done. Simple things such as bathing, going to the bathroom, getting dressed, or brushing my teeth all have to be done with the help of someone else. Chances are, when you get up every day and do these things, you don't even think about it. Simple actions throughout each day are automatic and often get taken for granted. I know I took them for granted.

But life can change in a split second. Jumping up out of bed was no more. Standing in the shower with the water running down over my head was a luxury of the past. Now I have bed baths, or if I take a shower, I have to lie flat on a special stretcher as soap and water are run over each individual limb. I can't even do something as simple as fix my own hair and makeup. Before my accident, when I hopped out of bed and got ready for the day, I never once thought, "What would I do if I couldn't do this for myself anymore?" Have you ever lain in bed and thought about how everything you do in a day, from sunup to sundown, would be accomplished if you had to depend on someone else to do it for you? Think about it. There are so many small details that go into your day. Many of the things you do every day are so routine that you do them without a second thought.

So, where do you find the strength and determination to press on and move forward when life, as you know it, has completely changed? As a sixteen-year-old, somewhere in the back of my mind, I must have wondered how I could go on. Adjusting to having someone else be my hands and feet was a struggle. The struggle led to frustration and a bad attitude. I learned the hard way that yelling at people (while my volume may not have come across as yelling, I'm sure my facial expressions did) didn't necessarily get the job done just how I wanted. Let's face it—it wasn't going to be perfect. My hair was a little different than I would fix it, or my clothes got put away in different places.

Then, I had to deal with the repercussions of hurting someone's feelings when my bad attitude was out of control. In the middle of trying circumstances, like most of us, I didn't take time to think and choose my words carefully; I just reacted, which often resulted in a response that was not the best. It's true that there's nothing normal about someone else having to do just about everything for you. Transitioning from everyday life walking to everyday life being paralyzed took time. It was a process. Somewhere inside, I had to find the God-given attitude that would help pull me through.

It's Worth It

When I was five years old, my mom told me not to do something—I don't even remember what it was—and my mom said I would get a spanking if I did it. Later, my mom found me doing the very thing that she had told me not to do. She asked me, "Jessica, if you knew you were going to get a spanking, why did you do it anyway?"

I replied, "Because it was worth it."

I was determined to do what I wanted to do, and no matter what the circumstances or consequences were, I was going to do it. While I, unfortunately, was using that determination for something negative at the age of five, I believe God placed that determination in me to help me get through the experience of being paralyzed. When one moment, the whole world is wide open for you to pursue whatever opportunity you wish, and the next moment, that world is rocked by dramatic change, you have to be determined. Somewhere inside, you have to dig deep and believe that life can and will go on. You have to believe that you were created on purpose and with purpose and that God's plan for you is a good one, even when you don't understand how something good could ever possibly come out of the situation you are facing. No matter what you are facing, God will equip you to pursue His purpose for your life.

The Word says that you are "fearfully and wonderfully made" (Ps. 139:14). It also says that God works all things together for your good (Rom. 8:28) and that God has good plans for you (Jer. 29:11). Whether you are in the middle of good times or tough times, you have to stand upon those truths.

While you may not be able to accomplish something a certain

way or even the way you planned, there are always other options. When you go through something tragic—and we all have our own stories—it's God who pulls you through. You may not believe it or even realize it, but God is right there with you in the midst

> *You have to believe that you were created on purpose and with purpose and that God's plan for you is a good one.*

of everything in your life. He's the one who gives you the determination to face your struggles head-on and make it through them. I was determined that my situation was not going to defeat me: I was determined that I would still be happy despite my disability, and every day, I am still determined that tomorrow will be better than yesterday. Keeping this mind-set and maintaining a positive attitude has helped me through the challenges that I face on a regular basis. Staying determined to figure out new ways of getting the job done kept me going and keeps me going. I will not let anything keep me from fulfilling my God-given purpose.

My determination, in a sense, gave me hope that things would be OK. When you allow a situation to make you depressed or overwhelm you with fear or doubt, it's as if you have already decided that the outcome can't be good, that you're doomed no matter what. But when you stay determined and hold tight to the truth that God's plan for you is good, you have tapped into your God-given strength, and you can press on, believing the outcome can and will be different. Even though I was paralyzed physically, I didn't have to be paralyzed emotionally or spiritually. I didn't have to be sad or upset because I knew life would still go on.

When I was five years old, I used that determination for something negative simply because I thought it was worth it. Isn't living life to the fullest and passionately pursuing God's

> *I will not let anything keep me from fulfilling my God-given purpose.*

plan for your life worth it? Isn't fulfilling the purpose you were created for worth summoning up some determination? Trust me, it's worth it.

Handling Emotions

Your emotions can run in all sorts of directions when tragedy strikes. Many quadriplegics I have met find the emotional side of being physically paralyzed is too much for them. They cannot handle the thought of not being able to move, and they allow their emotions to take over to the point that they wish they were either dead or mindless. When those emotions take over, people begin to slip away into dark places. It is heart-wrenching to see that happen to them. The physical paralysis consumes them like a disease, paralyzing not only their bodies but also their minds and spirits. Some even commit suicide. It is so tragic.

While I understand the challenges they face and have felt the same sense of loss, I never wanted to head into those dark places. I never understood how anyone could look at the beauty and majesty of God's creation and not realize that life is a precious gift. Every detail of creation speaks to the loving care and creativity of a God who loves us enough to give us a world that is a delight for the senses, from the songs of the birds in the sky to the beauty and fragrance of the roses growing in the backyard to the smooth taste of blueberry cheesecake. My life is full of blessings every day, both big and small, and they are evidence that my life is worth living. I made the choice early on that life was worth it, even if it no longer looked like what I once expected and dreamed of. I was so grateful to still be alive that the thought of living life paralyzed didn't really bother me. I knew life could and would go on, and that's all that mattered.

Since day one, I have overcome many things, but for some reason, I still had a tendency in certain areas to think my circumstances and my chair were beyond the power of God. While I didn't mind being paralyzed, I began to let my paralysis define me instead of just being who I always was, except I happened to be in a chair. While I know—and I tell myself—I'm still the same person, being paralyzed ended up lowering my confidence level over the years.

My emotional struggle came from the uncertainty associated with being in a chair rather than the lack of a will to live. I desired to live life to the fullest, but the chair and the paralysis had a way of making me feel ugly on the outside. Before my accident, I typically had a boyfriend. But afterward, dating came to a screeching halt. The boys I knew all scattered. I heard comments from old boyfriends like, "I want the old Jessica back; I can't be with you this way." Some of my friends also said things such as, "If you weren't in that chair, you'd still be dating." The rejection and the comments left me feeling jaded, and the chair seemed to become a burden of ugliness weighing on me.

In circumstances like that, emotions have a way of controlling your life in a different way. When you allow emotions to rule your mind and heart, you feel beaten down all the time. Whispers of disgust, despair, and defeat torment you, and you feel less than yourself. The thoughts of fear and worry consume you, and the emotions get rooted deeper and deeper inside. The deeper they get rooted, the harder they are to see and the harder they are to get control of.

You pretend everything is OK. You put a pretty smile on your face and go through life as if everything were perfect, but it's a front, a mask. On the inside, you're an emotional wreck.

Before my accident, I was confident and outgoing. But after the accident, the deeper I hid my feelings, the more reserved and un-sure I became. The confident person I once was began to disappear as a weak, emotion-controlled version of me began to take over. While I desired to still be confident, it felt easier to give in to the emotions. I let my emotions control me, but that is no way to live.

"I know that I am fearfully and wonderfully made.

I praise you, for I am fearfully and wonderfully made. Wonder-ful are your works; my soul knows it very well" (Psalm 139).

"I know that in God's eyes I am precious and beautiful... to give them beauty for ashes" (Isaiah 61:3, NKJV).

"As you come to him, a living stone rejected by men but in the sight of God chosen and precious..." (I Pet. 2:4).

"Behold, you are beautiful, my love" (Song of Solomon 1:16).

But even though I know these things, there were times when my thoughts and the lies from the devil continually filled my mind, telling me that my circumstances and my chair made me ugly and less than desirable. I also know that God's Word says it's not good for man to be alone (Genesis 2:18), but yet again, my circumstanc-es made me fear I would always be alone. I wondered if anyone could ever fall in love with me and marry me, even though I was in a chair. I let fear convince me that this chair would doom me to be single for the rest of my life.

Voicing my fears out loud was completely terrifying to me because hiding my feelings made them seem not so real. If I hid them behind the mask, then I still appeared to be the confident person I always was, giving a false sense that I was OK and nothing was wrong. I feared admitting my feelings because admitting them made me feel defeated by them. I did not want people to know my insecurities because I was afraid of what they would think. And I was also afraid it was what everyone else was thinking about me too. I needed to pretend I was strong, confident, and fine when, in reality, I was feeling anything but those things.

When I opened up more to the truth of what I was feeling, I discovered a very powerful weakness: I was worrying about what this world has to offer and seeking worldly rewards in order to feel important. I had somehow convinced myself that because my outside was broken, I was broken, too. The Word tells us that true beauty resides in the person living inside you (1 Pet. 3:3-4), but I had let my circumstances convince me otherwise. My focus was in the wrong place, and it kept me from living in freedom. I needed to find a way to really know who I was in God's eyes.

CHAPTER FOUR

Finding Freedom

What is it in life that keeps us so focused on appearance, material things, and overall comforts? TV shows and magazine articles dictate how life is "supposed" to go or how people are "supposed" to look. Why do we let other people or the media tell us what is ideal in life? We live in a culture where having a tall, dark, handsome husband, a nice house, a new BMW, and two or three kids is the "perfect" story for most women. I began to believe that those things were what I was supposed to have, and since I didn't have them, I convinced myself that the chair must be the problem.

But the truth is that I know a lot of single women who can walk but still have similar insecurities, the same fear that they will never find someone. Their insecurities come from other sources, such as their weight, other aspects of how they look, or other issues, some of which are deep heart issues. Then, on the flip side, I also have several friends who are quadriplegics and in a chair but are happily married. The chair has nothing to do with it. It is time to stop buying into the ideals that the world presents and instead buy into the truth of what God has to say.

Know Who You Are

Knowing who you really are in the sight of God is the first step in the battle. You need to know what God says about you. When you are a child of God, He makes you beautiful from the inside out. Ephesians 5:15-16 says, "Look carefully then how you walk, not as unwise but as wise, making the best use of the time." I was not making the most of my time because my time was consumed by worry and thoughts of the things I didn't have that the world said I should. I knew the truth, but I had a hard time letting it take root in my heart and my mind. I let what the world thought, and the circumstances of my condition control my emotions and define who I was.

I would think to myself over and over again that no one could ever want me because I was in a chair or that the chair made me undesirable. For years, I bought into the lie that the chair made me an unlikable, ugly person. Deep down, I knew it was a lie. Growing up in church and going to Sunday school, I was taught that God says I am beautiful. I was taught what the Word of God says about who I am. I was taught not to buy into the lies of anything or anyone that made me feel as if I were ugly or anything less than what God says about me. Those seeds of truth from the Word were planted deep in my mind and heart, but I had allowed lies to choke out their growth.

But how could I shift to believing the truth in God's Word and living life confident in God when all I seemed to know and believe were the lies in my mind? How could I become a woman fully committed to God when, even though it was what I wanted, it felt impossible? I needed to let God define what true beauty is.

First, I had to realize that it wasn't something that was just going to go away. I had to go through it; I was going through it for a reason, and I had to walk it

> *Knowing who you really are in the sight of God is the first step in the battle.*

out. James 1:2-4 says, "Consider it pure joy, my brothers and sisters, whenever you face trials of many kinds because you know that the testing of your faith produces perseverance. Let perseverance finish its work so that you may be mature and complete, not lacking anything" (NIV). Overcoming circumstances and pressing through things helps you grow and become more mature in your walk with Christ.

Everyone has to go through trials. Instead of feeling defeated by the trials, embrace them for what they are—an opportunity to grow. When you do that, a new you begins to rise up from the ashes, and the trial becomes easier and easier until, one day, it barely crosses your mind. Once I accepted the trial for what it was, I had to stop pretending I had no fear. Exposing a lie is the best way to stop it. When you continue to suppress your feelings deep inside in the darkness, hiding them for no one to see, it only gives them more power. Lies need to be exposed to light in order to be stopped. Jesus said, "I am…the truth" (John 14:6). He also said, "I am the light of the world" (John 8:12). When you bring your lies to the feet of Jesus, His light and His truth expose them as the lies they are. Lies flourish in the darkness but have to flee in the light. When you finally admit what you're feeling, the power of the lies is eliminated, and they no longer have control over you.

Believe me, I know it's hard and scary to even consider admitting the truth of what you are feeling, but being honest and 'fessing up does something powerful. You feel free and less tormented. The more lies are exposed to light, the harder it is for the darkness to get a foothold in the first place, until eventually, it doesn't even have a chance of getting in. But you can't rely on your own strength. 1 Chronicles 16:11 says, "Look to the LORD and his strength; seek his face always" (NIV). Seeking God and looking towards Him gives you strength to face the storms and trials of life.

> *Instead of feeling defeated by the trials, embrace them for what they are— an opportunity to grow.*

Fearfully and Wonderfully Made

My pivotal moment came when I took hold of God's strength, took a deep breath, and released the lies by giving my testimony at church. I was so scared to get up there in front of all those people and admit my deep, dark secrets and insecurities that I thought I was going to throw up. But I could no longer keep hiding and pretending I was a perfect, emotionally controlled person with no problems. Even as I approached the stage, the enemy was attacking my mind: What would people think? What if they think it's true that this chair does make me ugly?

While I was scared to death and dizzy and nauseated from fear, once I got up there and began to reveal the deep emotions that I had kept hidden for so long, a powerful release occurred inside me. I felt the weight of embarrassment lift off me, and the truth filled my mind, leaving no room for the lies.

But that was only the beginning. To keep the truth in my mind, I had to continually keep bringing the lies into the light. It was one thing to get up there on stage and admit it once, but I had to continually keep admitting it. I had to expose the lies and replace them with the truth on a daily basis. I had to take every thought captive.

"We destroy arguments and every lofty opinion raised against the knowledge of God, and take every thought captive to obey Christ" (2 Cor. 10:5).

John 8:31-32 says, "If you abide in My word, you are My disciples indeed. And you shall know the truth, and the truth shall make you free" (NKJV). When you release the insecurities and fears you have kept bottled inside all these years and replace the lies with the truth, true freedom in Christ is revealed. I told myself over and over that I am a precious child of God, worthy and capable, and that God loves me and thinks I'm beautiful. I also repeated Scripture verses in my mind to remind me of the truth:

"I praise you, for I am fearfully and wonderfully made" (Ps. 139:14).

"The LORD your God has chosen you...for his treasured possession" (Deut. 7:6).

Doing this repeatedly began to shift my thinking. I was discovering my identity as a child of God, but I had to keep the truth continually in mind in order to maintain my freedom. Psalm 139:11-16 says, "If I say, 'Surely the darkness will hide me and the light become night around me,' even the darkness will not be dark to you; the night will shine like the day, for darkness is as light to you. For you created my inmost being; you knit me together in my mother's womb. I praise you because I am fearfully and wonderfully made; your works are wonderful. I know that full well. My frame was not hidden from you when I was made in the secret place. When I was woven together in the depths of the earth, your eyes saw my unformed body. All the days ordained for me were written in your book before one of them came to be."

> *When you release the insecurities and fears you have kept bottled inside all these years and replace the lies with the truth, true freedom in Christ is revealed.*

The accident, my chair, my circumstances—none of them were a surprise to God. All the days ordained for me were written in His book before one of them came to be. This chair does not define me; God does. What other people think does not define me; God does. My identity comes from Him, and no matter where your insecurities lie, that's true for you too. God is more powerful than anything you are going through or feeling. Seek the truth of who you are in Him. Write His Word on your heart. Take every thought captive to the obedience of Christ, and walk in the freedom Jesus died to give you. Don't stay bound up in the lies. God paid a high price for your freedom, so don't stay imprisoned by the lies.

I admit that it took years for me to feel normal again. It was a process because I had allowed the lies to take root in my heart. Lies, bitterness, unforgiveness, and all the negative things we allow into our hearts are like the roots of weeds trying to force out any healthy growth in your soul. If you just deal with the parts that show on the surface, the roots dig down deeper, and the weeds spring right up again. You have to dig all that junk out of your heart and allow God to fill the empty spots with His love, grace, mercy, peace, joy, and all the other good gifts He has for you. You need to be "rooted and built up in [Jesus]" (Col. 2:7), "rooted and grounded in love" (Eph. 3:17). You have to let Him heal the hurts you have been carrying around for so long, so that beautiful new things can flourish. God had to heal me on the inside from past hurts and fill my heart and mind with the fact I am beautiful simply because I'm His child. I had to believe that was what really mattered.

I read once that, similar to our physical muscles, we have spiritual muscles—our hearts and minds. To keep our hearts and minds spiritually fit, we must exercise them by reading God's Word, praying, and keeping a godly perspective in everyday life. I also have to exercise my spiritual muscles by spending time in the presence of the Lord, sitting at His feet, worshipping Him, and thanking Him for the blessings in my life. Psalm 40:1-3 says, "I waited patiently for the LORD; he inclined to me and heard my cry. He drew me up from the pit of destruction, out of the miry bog, and set my feet

> *You have to dig all that junk out of your heart and allow God to fill the empty spots with His love, grace, mercy, peace, joy, and all the other good gifts He has for you.*

upon a rock, making my steps secure. He put a new song in my mouth, a song of praise to our God. Many will see and fear and put their trust in the LORD."

When we stop exercising our spiritual muscles, our spirits grow weak because we don't have the tools we need to handle life free of fear, worry, insecurity, and uncertainty. When I don't exercise my spiritual muscles daily, weaknesses creep back into my life, and I forget the awesome power I have in God. God is the source of my strength (Ps. 28:7). When I am open with Him about my weaknesses, I am made strong (2 Cor. 12:10). And where God is, there is no darkness. Darkness cannot exist where there is light, and Jesus is the light (John 1:4-9). He is the light of the world (John 8:12). His Word is a lamp to my feet and a light to my path (Ps. 119:105). The darkness of the lies in my mind is easily overcome when I bring them into the presence of the Lord when I stay focused on Him instead of my circumstances or my chair.

The more I abandon my emotions to God, the more peace of mind I have. He lifted me out of the ditch, sat me on a solid rock, and taught me how to praise Him. And it's "not that I have already obtained all this, or have already arrived at my goal, but I press on to take hold of that for which Christ Jesus took hold of me" (Phil. 3:12, NIV). I am working toward that day when I will finally be all that God created me to be. I am not there yet, but I will keep pressing toward the goal.

"But one thing I do: forgetting what lies behind and straining forward to what lies ahead, I press on toward the goal for the prize of the upward call of God in Christ Jesus" (Phil. 3:13-14).

It's a gradual process, and God is working on me on the inside every day. God tells us we are beautiful crowns of jewels just because we are His children.

"You shall be a crown of beauty in the hand of the LORD" (Is. 62:3).

I found a way to let myself be OK with being physically broken because it was that brokenness that made me feel less than myself. In reality, I'm not broken at all—my body may be, but my body doesn't make me who I am. I know even in this chair that God has a plan for my life, and I believe if I follow His will, it will be an abundant life far better than I could ever hope for, think, or imagine. And it is all for His glory.

"For I know the plans I have for you, declares the LORD, plans for welfare and not for evil, to give you a future and a hope. Then you will call upon me and come and pray to me, and I will hear you. You will seek me and find me, when you seek me with all your heart" (Jer. 29:11-13).

"I came that they may have life and have it abundantly" (John 10:10).

"Now to him who is able to do far more abundantly than all that we ask or think, according to the power at work within us, to him be glory in the church and in Christ Jesus throughout all generations, forever and ever. Amen" (Eph. 3:20-21).

Just Be You

While being a quadriplegic was clearly not an ideal situation, I found new ways to do things and to get around, even though I had physical limitations; new ways to feel independent, even though truly being independent felt impossible; new ways of feeling beautiful, even though sometimes feeling beautiful was the furthest thing from my mind. I had to be persistent in redirecting my mind to the fact that life was worth it. I had to be persistent in taking captive every thought that went against that truth and bringing my thoughts into alignment with the truth.

Even when I found myself facing something that seemed impossible, I stayed determined that somehow I would still get it done. Having independence in some areas definitely made it more tolerable in the areas I didn't, but at times, even though I was learning how to deal with it, I still felt as if I had no control at all. I had this strange feeling as if my body were not really my own. The more I sat back and let people just do things for me however they wanted, the less I felt like myself. If you don't stay grounded and focused on what you can do and who you really are, you can easily lose sight of the real you.

God made you the way He did on purpose. Knowing who you are in Him is the key to being the real you. When you let Jesus define you, all the ways the world tries to define you, all the labels people try to stick on you, and all the baggage and burdens, the enemy tries to weigh you down with start to lose their power. It frees you to just be you, the real you: the fearfully- and-wonderfully-made you, the redeemed you, the all-things-new you, the accepted you, the forgiven you, the chosen you, the friend-of-God you, the child-of-the-Lord-Most-High you.

While depending on people is a necessity when you are paralyzed, I had to find a balance so I could still feel like myself. I finally discovered I could still keep a handle on my life in specific ways. Even though I don't always feel like it, my body is still my own. Even though I can't give myself my medicine, I still pay attention to what is being put in my mouth. Even though I can't change my own bandage, I can ask those helping me what they are doing every step of the way and ask them to stop if something makes me uncomfortable. Even though I can't dress myself, I can still pick out my clothes and make sure they look right to me once I'm dressed. The ability to choose and make your own decisions is a big part of freedom.

The people taking care of me may find it obnoxious sometimes. They may even think that I don't trust them, but that is not the case. Paying attention to what goes on with me and my body is the only control I have in certain circumstances. And even with the best intentions, things can get mixed up or go wrong. I absolutely know God is with me and is protecting me along the way, but I also know He gave me a mind with the ability to think and understand. My body may be paralyzed, but my mind isn't. I am not going to let the paralysis spread. I want to be an active participant in my own life, not a passive one. Sitting there quietly like a bump on a log and letting anyone do any old thing to me would be giving in to the paralysis and giving up.

> *When you let Jesus define you, all the ways the world tries to define you, all the labels people try to stick on you, and all the baggage and burdens the enemy tries to weigh you down with start to lose their power.*

While paying attention to what goes on with me is important, finding the balance between when to say something and when to sit back and watch is just as necessary. I'm still not all that good at the sit-back-and-watch part. Before my accident, I was a get-up-and-take-charge kind of person.

I didn't ask for help much. I even did things like rearranging the heavy, old, solid wood furniture in my bedroom all by myself.

The change from being like that to boom, having no control at all, was definitely a humbling experience. I guess that's why I say too much sometimes.

Although some days are more difficult than others, I have continued to find the strength to press through. I know for a fact that if it weren't for God, I wouldn't still be here today. As I began to embrace the new ways I had to do things and adjusted my expectations, I discovered it wasn't as bad as I thought it was. While I may be chained physically, I am not chained in any other way, and the sense of freedom that surrounds me despite my circumstances is amazing. You may be in a similar situation. There may be circumstances in your life that seem like physical chains. But the Word of God promises that "if the Son sets you free, you will be free indeed" (John 8:36). Don't lose sight of that. Even in the midst of the most challenging circumstances, you can have spiritual and emotional freedom.

The Word also says, "For freedom Christ has set us free" (Gal. 5:1). That means the purpose of your Christ-purchased freedom is freedom. So don't put on chains that were never meant to shackle you or pick up burdens you were never meant to bear. Jesus said, "Come to me, all you who are weary and burdened, and I will give you rest....My yoke is easy and my burden is light" (Matt. 11:28, 30). When you are feeling chained up or weighed down, go to Jesus. Go to the foot of the cross. Let Jesus take your cares, your worries, your anxious thoughts, your chains, and your burdens. Let Him give you His rest. Whenever I start to worry about something, or I feel weighed down by cares, I just bring whatever it is to the foot of the cross. I know God can and will take care of it, and He will take care of you, too.

Being paralyzed has become my new normal, and tasks have

become easier. I was able to get into a routine that seemed some-what natural. It's been twenty-nine years, and while there are al-ways days that are better than others, I like the new normal. It's not something I resent or despise. I'm still the same old me; I just have to function and get around a little differently.

So, let God define who you are. I can honestly tell you from my experience that finally finding that freedom is powerful! Knowing you are beautiful just the way you are brings a sense of peace and comfort. So cling to that knowledge, and let God show you His plans for your life. Make the pursuit of His will your primary fo-cus. Don't let your emotions control you. Exercise those spiritual muscles, and take every thought captive to the obedience of Christ. Jesus is the light, and He will never be overcome by the darkness of even your deepest emotions. So run to Him. Let His light shine in your darkness and expose the lies. And then hold fast to the truth that you are His. You are beautiful. You are fearfully and wonder-

> *Don't put on chains that were never meant to shackle you or pick up burdens you were never meant to bear.*

fully made. You are chosen. You are accepted. You are a child of God, and no one can ever snatch you from His hand.

CHAPTER FIVE

Faith Arises

People often ask me, "How do you do it? How can you stay so happy and motivated when you're paralyzed?"

Honestly, my initial response to these kinds of questions is, "How do I do what?" I live my life just like everyone else. I breathe in and breathe out, I wake up every day, just like you do, and I continue the routine of my life. Having a life worth living and an abundant life full of joy has nothing to do with whether you can walk.

You may think it's rude or unkind for someone to ask me something like this, but I don't mind. It gives me opportunities to speak the truth about what some people call an impossible situation. And that is what they're saying when they ask me questions like that. They look at my life and think it would be impossible for them. But the truth is that with God nothing is impossible (Luke 1:37). God created each of us with a specific purpose, and as long as we are on this earth, we still have a purpose. One day, an afternoon drive changed my whole world, but I survived. I was spared for a reason. God doesn't do things by accident. There must be a purpose.

One day, you walk around and move, but the next day, you can't move anything except your head and your neck. You begin to think. You start to wonder. You reflect on life and what it's all about, and you start to see what is really important. Suddenly, small things become so significant. I typically ignored the little things in life before my accident. My thoughts were tied up with the latest dramatic episode of high school life or the material things I thought I couldn't live without.

I was focused on things that really weren't important at all. It happens to many people all over the world every day. We get consumed by stuff and the everyday events of life that don't really matter in the long run. Before my accident, I was both in the world and of the world, but that is not what God has called us to be.

"And do not be conformed to this world, but be transformed by the renewing of your mind, that you may prove what is that good and acceptable and perfect will of God" (Rom. 12:2, NKJV).

"They are in the world…[but] they are not of the world, just as I am not of the world" (John 17:11, 14).

Plans and Purposes

As a teenager, I thought life couldn't get any better. While I, of course, had some of the typical teenage issues, I thought life was great just the way it was. I grew up in a good home. My parents taught me about life and faith and what they meant. Faith was never something that was forced upon me; instead, it always was encouraged gently. My dad never was a big churchgoer, but my mom and I always went. I loved Sunday school and all the things I learned about the Bible. I even enjoyed going to church every week.

But while I enjoyed it, going to church was more about routine and doing the right thing than about worshipping God, learning about Him and His Word, or building a relationship with Him. I typically spent my Sunday mornings at church sitting in the balcony with my friends, giggling and passing notes written on the bulletins, with the sermon just being background noise during the fun.

The Lord meant a lot to me, but pursuing Him or His plan for me wasn't my purpose in life. My purpose was tied up with my ideas of what I thought I needed or wanted at the time, and I let those things define me. But I was missing the mark. The truth is that God created each of us with a special purpose. Each of us is a masterpiece of God's creation, made to fulfill a specific plan that God came up with long before we were ever born. You were perfectly designed for your purpose.

"For we are his workmanship, created in Christ Jesus for good works, which God prepared beforehand, that we should walk in them" (Eph. 2:10).

Here's the thing: instead of following God's plan for my life, I had my own plan, and I expected God to fit into it. It was all about me and the things I wanted or thought I had to have to be happy. Then, my so-called plan was interrupted, and I woke up in a hospital, paralyzed from the shoulders down.

I am not in the least bit saying it was God's fault. I know interruptions happen in life that can take us down hard, rocky roads, and I also know and believe with all my heart that when they do, God always works it out for good. Romans 8:28 says, "And we know that God causes everything to work together for the good of those who love God and are called according to his purpose for them."

I truly believe that! It may sometimes take years and years for someone to finally see the good in what has happened, but one day, it will be revealed. I didn't wake up after my accident, and the next day, think positive, happy-go-lucky thoughts to myself. It took time to go through the emotions. When I first woke up and became aware of my accident, all I was concerned about were my original plans I had been so excited about. Then, once reality began to set in, all I was focused on was learning how to adjust and adapt to the new lifestyle I had been presented with.

After the initial shock of it all began to wear off, I was left with just my thoughts. High school drama didn't matter anymore, and neither did material things. Living life able-bodied, I always had a sense of control over my life. I thought I had all the answers, and I thought I had it all figured out. But suddenly, I was left with what felt like no control at all. For months I allowed that feeling of lack of control to paralyze my mind. I spent time just sitting, staring off at nothing and wondering about life. While I had pressed forward with some independence by going back to school and getting out some, I kept finding that my physical and emotional fear still made me afraid to get back to the land of the living and go on big adventures like I used to.

As months passed by and my faith began to grow, small bits of that fear began to chip off. As I took baby steps out into the world, I discovered that life does go on, whether you decide to keep participating in it or not. If I chose to, I could look at the brighter side and still make something of my life and move on.

It took about a year, but finally, a small glimpse of courage began to peep out of me, and I went on my first vacation since my accident. My sister Cara and I were headed to Florida. My mom was scared to death to let me go all the way to Florida with just my sister and a nurse, but my grandfather convinced her it was a good idea. We were headed to a Campus Crusade conference at Disney World in Orlando. I promise you, at the time, I was far more interested in Disney World than some Christian conference.

When we arrived, I was so excited to do something fun and have some adventures. We headed to the park and had a fun-filled day. After missing 80 percent of the conference, I finally unwillingly and begrudgingly agreed to go to one of the meetings. I thought to myself, "Oh my word. This is going to be so boring. Can we please just go play?" But you know what? As I sat there, something happened. It was as if a light bulb went off in my head. That day, as I listened to what they had to say, I realized I wasn't living a lifestyle bearing witness to my confession that Jesus was my Lord.

While the conference truly was eye-opening at that moment, when I got home, not much changed. Don't get me wrong; some small changes happened, but for the most part, everything was still about me rather than my relationship with God. While I thought I had this big epiphany after my accident and let God take the wheel, I really hadn't. Instead I still tried to control everything around me by making plans and believing that God was going to fit into them.

I do believe it's great to plan ahead, get focused, and be purposeful in life, but I also believe God, not you, should be in charge of those plans. When you can't tell which direction God wants you to go, just take baby steps in doing the next right thing. Gradually, you'll see that even though it doesn't feel like it, He's guiding those steps too. Sometimes, it is necessary to just go through stuff.

The Book of Isaiah says, "And your ears shall hear a word behind you, saying, 'This is the way, walk in it,' when you turn to the right or when you turn to the left" (30:21). But the thing is that you have to listen when God tells you which way to go. I needed to work on that. For years, I continued going around the same mountains over and over, relearning the same lessons and hitting different obstacles because I refused to pay attention to the signs God kept showing me. I refused to listen.

Stop Swimming

After about eight years, I finally realized I needed to wake up and get a clue! God doesn't want you to fit Him into your plan; He wants you to build your life around His plan for you. Right then and there, at that moment, I knew I had a choice. I didn't have to change. But I chose to change because I knew if Jesus lived in me, I would want to change. Galatians 5:24-25 says, "Those who belong to Christ Jesus have nailed the passions and desires of their sinful nature to his cross and crucified them there. Since we are living by the Spirit, let us follow the Spirit's leading in every part of our lives" (NLT).

As I read that passage of Scripture, I thought, "OK, that's pretty straightforward. It clearly states every part of our lives." That means we need to follow the Spirit's leading in how we communicate, what we think, what we feel, how we act, and every other thing about our lives. While it sounded simple enough, my strong will made it hard.

It is so crazy how my flesh puts up a fight. If you've ever watched Joyce Meyer, you may have seen this act that she does where she moves around like a robot and repeats over and over, "What about me? What about me? What about me? What about me?"[1] It's really quite hilarious, but in reality, it is so true. We all get so wrapped up in "What about me?" that we lose sight of what is really important. We lose sight of what our true purpose is. We lose sight of the abundant life that we are supposed to be living as we fulfill God's plans for us.

When I hit my thirties, I began to realize many different things. I could see where I had grown and changed over the years, but I was still fighting against the flow of life. When I finally recognized that, God gave me an analogy, and I wrote down these words that came to my mind:

> I'm a thirty-one-year-old quadriplegic. I can't move a limb of my body, yet I find myself swimming. I'm in this big, huge ocean we call life, and I can see land far, far off in the distance. I keep swimming and kicking, trying to get there, but the harder I swim, the farther the land seems to get. So I fight harder and swim faster, but I never get there. I cry out to the Lord, "Why, God? Why? I don't understand. I'm trying so hard. What's wrong? Why can't I get there?"
>
> And the Lord said to me, "Baby girl, STOP! Stop swimming. It may feel like if you stop trying, you will sink and drown, falling way down into the depths of the unknown ocean. But as you begin to sink, if you just look up, you'll see I'm right here with you. I've been right there with you the whole time, just waiting for you to stop trying to do this on your own and look up and realize I'm right there. Reach out to Me, and I will scoop you up and carry you over those waves of life and sit you on that land, safe and dry. Yes, there are huge waves and vicious storms, but I've got you. I will protect you and lead you to the land."

I suddenly realized that every breath I took and every day that I woke up and lived was a gift from God. He was right there with me the whole time. As I witnessed miracle after miracle occur in my life, I felt the presence of the Lord grow stronger day by day. Psalm 144:4 says, "Man is like a breath; his days are like a passing shadow." So if that's true, then all this stuff you and I go through trying to make ourselves happy is nothing but a mere shadow. How sad would it be to miss out on something bigger? something better? something that will truly fulfill you? I don't know about you, but I want the best God has for me. I want to live my life 100 percent lined up in perfect alignment with His plan and purpose for me.

I know you may be thinking, "Well, that's impossible. Who can live a perfect life with no blemish or flaw?" And you're right—that is impossible! But it is not about being perfect. Just because I am committed to following God's plan for my life doesn't mean I don't sin. Just because I'm a Christian, it doesn't mean that I don't mess up, miss the mark, fall short, or make a mistake. Romans 3:23 clearly says, "For everyone has sinned; we all fall short of God's glorious standard" (NLT).

So, yes, we all are human, and we all make mistakes, but something huge happened when I decided to make Jesus the ruler and Lord over my life! This desire came over me to do the best I can in life, believing that because of the shed blood of Jesus, I can change. I can allow Jesus to make me better. I can allow Him to work in and through me to make me more like Him. And the more I become like Jesus, the more I am able to live my life 100 percent lined up in perfect alignment with God's plan and purpose for me. As I started to really let Jesus be the Lord of my life, as I surrendered my will to His and began to seek His plan for me instead of trying to fit God into my plan for me, I began to change. My relationship with God grew stronger and stronger—and it is still growing!

I now want to walk with God every day. I want to have the fruit of His Spirit—"love, joy, peace, patience, kindness, goodness,

> *I don't want to waste the precious time God has given me on this earth in pursuit of things that aren't part of His perfect will for my life.*

faithfulness, gentleness, self-control" (Gal 5:22-23)—at work in my life. I want to live a life of devotion to God, just as Titus 2:11-14 (NLT) says:

For the grace of God has been revealed, bringing salvation to all people. And we are instructed to turn from godless living and sinful pleasures. We should live in this evil world with wisdom, righteousness, and devotion to God, while we look forward with hope to that wonderful day when the glory of our great God and Savior, Jesus Christ, will be revealed. He gave his life to free us from every kind of sin, to cleanse us, and to make us his very own people, totally committed to doing good deeds.

You see when I didn't have a real relationship with God, it was all about me and my plan and what I could get out of this life and from this world. But my accident has taught me that life is both short and precious! I don't want to waste the precious time God has given me on this earth in pursuit of things that aren't part of His perfect will for my life. God created me on purpose and with purpose, and I want to fulfill that purpose. I want to continue to change, to turn away from "godless living and sinful pleasures." And because of the grace of God at work in my life, I can do just that. I can listen for that voice that says, "This is the way, walk in it" (Isa. 30:21). I can choose to stop swimming and trying to do everything in my own power and instead let the Spirit of God lead and guide me, bringing me safely to the promised land of God's perfect will for my life.

Do I still sin? Yes. Do I mess up, miss the mark, fall short, or make a mistake? Absolutely. But when I do, I can find the grace and mercy I need at the foot of the cross of Jesus. I can freely ask for and freely receive forgiveness. I can have peace with God and peace in my heart, knowing that my sins have been wiped clean by my Savior. I can boldly approach the throne of grace with the confidence of a beloved daughter, knowing my heavenly Father loves me beyond compare.

Ecclesiastes 6:12 (NASB) says, "For who knows what is good for a man during his lifetime, during the few years of his futile life?

> *Life is not about being full of things of this world or whether I can walk or move. Life is about having a relationship with God and living to glorify Him.*

He will spend them like a shadow. For who can tell a person what will happen after him under the sun?" Between discovering that this life we live is nothing more than a mere shadow and experiencing a brush with death because of my accident, I realized that the bottom line is there is no meaning in life apart from God. Life is not about being full of things of this world or whether I can walk or move. Life is about having a relationship with God and living to glorify Him. That is my ultimate purpose here on this earth—and it's your purpose, too.

Jesus Himself said, "Beware! Guard against every kind of greed. Life is not measured by how much you own....Yes, a person is a fool to store up earthly wealth but not have a rich relationship with God" (Luke 12:15, 21). I now know true happiness doesn't come from what the world has to offer me, from the stuff I own, or from being able to walk but from the eternal realities found in Christ. Having a rich relationship with God is the true treasure. It is the key to a life of purpose. It is the only real source of peace, joy, and contentment.

Open Doors

A few years ago, I watched a movie called Facing the Giants. If you haven't seen it, please take some time to watch it. It's a definite must-see. It's a low-budget film, admittedly, with acting that could be better, but the message behind it is truly profound. The basic gist of the movie is that you can face any giant with God because nothing is impossible for Him. There are so many nuggets of truth throughout the whole movie that it would be too difficult to speak of all of them, which is why I recommend seeing it.

> *Having a rich relationship with God is the true treasure.*

There was one particular part that really spoke to me about

my paralysis. A prayer warrior named Mr. Bridges comes into the office of the main character and says, "Revelation chapter says 3 we serve a God that opens doors that no one can shut, and He shuts doors that no one can open. He says, 'Behold, I have placed before you an open door that no one can shut. I know you have a little strength, yet you have keep My word and have not denied My name.'"[2]

Being paralyzed may seem impossible to some, but being paralyzed has opened doors for me that would have never been opened had I not been in this situation. It's opened my eyes to new possibilities that I never dreamed were possible, enabling me to truly know without a doubt that with God, all things are possible. Even though I'm slow to learn and I'm a sinner, God is always there patiently, waiting to have a relationship with me! And while my strength may be small, I serve an all-powerful God who says, "Not by might, nor by power, but by my Spirit" (Zech. 4:6). I don't need to rely on my own strength to go through the doors God opens for me. I can rely on the Spirit to get me to and through every open door that is part of God's plan for my life.

God has a plan for paralyzed, broken, sinful me, and I want to fit my life around His plan, not the other way around. Even though my plan was interrupted, it's okay because I know God will give me nothing but His best. I want my life to glorify Him, and I want to live according to His plan! Yes, I screw up. Yes, it can be hard, but I know God is with me, and He will not give up on me. It's just as Philippians 1:6 (NIV) says, "Being confident of this, that he who began a good work in you will carry it on to completion until the day of Christ Jesus."

This accident happened for a reason, and I believe that reason can be summed up in Philippians 1:12, "I want you to know, brothers, that what has happened to me has really served to advance the gospel."

It's all good! And I thank Jesus for the opportunity to live and serve Him!

CHAPTER SIX

Triumph Over Defeat

Learning to drive my chair was the beginning of my story of triumphing over fear and learning to navigate my world in a new way. I continued to face challenges that I had to meet head-on. Whenever setbacks or attacks from the enemy happen that make me feel defeated, hopeless, and as if I will never have a meaningful, successful life, I have to know how to win the battle. I have to know how to triumph over defeat. I have to know that because of Jesus, I am more than a conqueror.

I was an outpatient at Eastside Medical Center to get IV antibiotics for a kidney infection. I was having very bad back pain (even though I am paralyzed, I still feel pain in my body, such as back pain or stomach aches). As they were stretching me to help relieve my back pain, my hip broke. No one, including me, had realized that my bones had become so fragile. I could feel that something was wrong, but I couldn't tell what. At first, I thought I was having an anxiety attack. I began to feel as if I couldn't breathe. I went from the outpatient floor to the ER and checked myself in. When the triage nurse checked my oxygen level, it was so low that they took me back immediately and put me on oxygen to help me breathe.

They admitted me to the hospital, but they couldn't figure out what was wrong, so my mom had me transferred to another hospital. A physician's assistant from Shepherd came to see me, and she was the one who finally figured it out. She had them take X-rays, which showed that my hip was broken. The broken hip caused a fat embolism, which moved to my lung and caused breathing difficulties. I was treated for the embolism, and I had to have surgery to repair my broken hip. I was in the hospital for about a week.

Time to Triumph

I have had physical setbacks like this happen to me quite a few times, but God is always watching out for me. The fact that I can still feel pain is a blessing that allows me to know what is going on in my body. And God has always made sure that when the enemy comes against me to try to defeat me, I am positioned where I can get the physical help I need (if I hadn't been in the hospital as an outpatient when `the embolism occurred and moved to my lung, I could have died).

So, no matter how many times Satan attacks me, I am going to keep pushing forward. I am not going to give up. My life has purpose, and as long as God keeps me on this earth, I am going to keep glorifying Him for the things He has done and pursuing His calling on my life.

"Now thanks be to God who always leads us in triumph in Christ, and through us diffuses the fragrance of His knowledge in every place" (2 Cor. 2:14).

God gives each of us different gifts to use to build His kingdom and to benefit the body of Christ. I believe that God has given me the spiritual gift of exhortation.

"Having gifts that differ according to the grace given to us, let us use them: if prophecy, in proportion to our faith; if service, in our serving; the one who teaches, in his teaching; the one who exhorts, in his exhortation; the one who contributes, in generosity; the one who leads, with zeal; the one who does acts of mercy, with cheerfulness" (Rom. 12:6-8).

I know that being in a chair is part of His plan to help me use the gift of exhortation to the best of my ability. When I talk to people about facing adversity, my words often carry more weight with them than the words of someone able-bodied would. You only have to look at me to know that I have faced some serious challenges. But I have not let those challenges defeat me. Yes, I have weaknesses, both physical and of other natures, but God promises that in my weakness, He is strong (2 Cor. 12:10). His power has given me everything I need that pertains to life and godliness (2 Pet. 1:3).

> *Each time I fight another battle and win and testify to others of the awesome power of God to save and uphold, it spreads the fragrance of Jesus to a world that is greatly in need of Him.*

And the most wonderful thing about triumphing over every plan of the enemy is the side effects it produces. When I triumph over the enemy, whether in a small thing or a big thing, it brings glory to God. It enables me to praise Him for all the great things He has done. And each triumph is a reminder of how much God loves me, allowing me to enjoy my relationship with Him all the more. In addition to that, every triumph, every victory in the face of defeat, helps spread the knowledge of the love and power of God to the people around me. Each time I fight another battle and win and testify to others of the awesome power of God to save and uphold, it spreads the fragrance of Jesus to a world that is greatly in need of Him.

Time to Hope

No matter what your circumstances are, you need to trust God to carry you through it. He is never going to let you go, especially in the face of difficult times.

Always maintain hope. Study after study has shown that hope has positive effects on health, academic performance, personal development, and happiness, among other things. One study, specifically of patients who experienced spinal cord injuries, found that "experiences of hope were important to all participants, providing energy and power to the process of struggling because hope is necessary for further progress and personal development."[1] Hope is important, no matter the challenges you are facing.

The Word of God teaches us the importance of hope, too. It also shows us where to place our hope: in God. Verse after verse talks about hoping in the Lord (e.g., Ps. 42:5; 1 Pet. 1:21). But beyond hoping in God, our hope is God. Psalm 71:5 says, "For you, O LORD, are my hope." One of God's names is the Hope of Israel (Jer. 14:8), and Romans 15:13 speaks of the "God of hope."

You need to persevere to find hope in every situation. In every circumstance, you need to look for the positive, the glimmer of hope. It is always there because God is with you, and He is hope. You can always find hope because God's Word promises that all things work together for the good of those who love Him (Rom. 8:28). The Word also promises that hope will not disappoint us:

"Now hope does not disappoint, because the love of God has been poured out in our hearts by the Holy Spirit who was given to us" (Rom. 5:5, NKJV).

By training yourself to look for the positive aspects of every situation you face, it helps to keep you from dwelling on the negative. It helps keep the enemy from being able to hit the target when he shoots fiery darts of lies at your mind and heart. It helps keep your focus on Jesus, the author and finisher of your faith. It enables you to run with endurance the race God has set before you.

Words of Life

To move to a place of triumph and stay there, even in the midst of troubles and trials, you need to be mindful of the words you are hearing and speaking. Positive, encouraging, and uplifting words will move you forward, propel you on, and keep you focused on the right things. Negative, discouraging words will only inhibit you and bring you down. And you need to make sure you know the difference between the two. Be choosy about what you let into your heart and mind, and be choosy about the words you let come out of your mouth from your mind and heart. The Word of God tells us that "death and life are in the power of the tongue" (Prov. 18:21). And in Deuteronomy 30:19 (NIV), the Lord told the people of Israel this, "I have set before you life and death, blessings and curses. Now choose life, so that you and your children may live."

You have a choice. You have a choice about the kinds of things you will allow in your life. You can choose blessings, or you can choose curses. You can choose life, or you can choose death. And

God wants you to choose life. He wants you to choose to really live the abundant life He has for you. He wants you to choose to listen to words of life that bring blessing, and He wants you to choose to speak those same words of life over yourself and everyone else you come into contact with. He wants you to choose to speak life. Life is worth it, but it is up to you to choose it.

A drive on a rainy afternoon changed my life in such a way that many would consider my life now to not be worth it. But they would be wrong. My life is worth it, and I choose and will continue to choose to live it for the glory of God. And I will use my gift of exhortation to speak life and blessings to the people God brings into my life. My words are powerful, and I want them to be life-giving, encouraging words that build people up rather than tear them down. And if my words in this book have encouraged you in any way, then you are one more piece of evidence that my life is worth it—and yours is, too.

> ### *Life is worth it, but it is up to you to choose it.*

When you are persevering in pursuit of God's plan for your life, don't let setbacks make you quit. Setbacks happen. They happen to all of us. But a setback is not a failure. It may be a step back, a step in the wrong direction, or even a fall, but you need to pick yourself back up, dust yourself off, and get back in the race. Never give up! Keep moving forward, one step at a time. You can make it, but only if you don't quit. Your life is worth it. You are worth it! God will give you the strength that you need to continue. He will light your path and show the way to the finish line.

"We have peace with God through our Lord Jesus Christ....

And not only this, but we also celebrate in our tribulations, knowing that tribulation brings about perseverance; and perseverance, proven character; and proven character, hope; and hope does not disappoint, because the love of God has been poured out within our hearts through the Holy Spirit who was given to us" (Rom. 5:1-5, NASB).

How God Plays a Part

When I look back at my life and everything that has happened, I can see God's hand at work every step of the way. He is behind my triumph over everything the enemy used to try to defeat me. We tend to view negative things that happen as only negative, but the truth is that we serve a God who promises to work all things together for our good. Sometimes, He allows something negative to happen in order for an even bigger positive to occur. I have seen this happen over and over again in my life.

Several years ago, I got really sick and was hospitalized for a bowel obstruction. They needed to put a tube down my nose to relieve the gas pressure, and to do so, they gave me a drug to help me relax and reduce my anxiety about the procedure. I am very sensitive to the drug because it can suppress my respiration, giving me a difficult time breathing. Because of that, I told them I could only receive a very small dose

Never give up! Keep moving forward, one step at a time. You can make it, but only if you don't quit. Your life is worth it. You are worth it!

of the drug and could only take it for the one procedure. Somehow, that very important nugget of information got lost, and they kept giving me one dose after another.

The next day, my breathing was extremely labored, but my nurse assumed I was OK because they were monitoring my vitals at the nurses' station. But that afternoon, my pulmonologist from Shepherd stopped by to see me. He took one look at me and went to the nurses' station to check my vitals. He was shocked to find my oxygen saturation level was down to 30. Anything below 90 is considered low, and anything below 60 indicates a need for supplemental oxygen.

My doctor called a code, and everyone rushed in to revive my nearly lifeless body. They placed me on a ventilator to help me breathe, and several hours later, after the drugs wore off, I came to. While the overall situation was scary, and I came close to dying, God was using it to reveal much bigger problems going on with my lungs. My left lung was actually partially collapsed, and my CO_2 levels were extremely high, among other issues. I had known something was wrong with my breathing for a while, but I had been ignoring it.

God knew that I needed help with my lungs, and rather than let me head down a destructive path on my own, He stepped in and saved me. My bowel obstruction, which actually cleared up on its own, was a negative that turned into an even bigger positive. This was another reminder that He is there guiding me, and I can most definitely trust Him. He is leading me in triumph, even when my circumstances seem like anything but triumphant. I can have hope, knowing that God has me in the palm of His hand, and He is always and ever will be working things together for my good.

How You Can Have Hope

To have true hope, you have to know where true hope is found. And it is found in Jesus Christ.

The dictionary defines hope in a couple of different ways. Hope can mean "to cherish a desire with anticipation; to want something to happen or be true."[2] This kind of hope makes me think of when you hoped for a pony for your birthday or the way you might have hoped to go to Disney World when you were a kid.

> *With Jesus as your source of true hope, you can be bold and courageous because there is nothing to fear.*

Whether you were likely to receive a pony or go to Disney World didn't really matter. You still cherished the hope that it would happen and longed for it to happen.

Hope also means "to desire with expectation of obtainment or fulfillment." This is closer to the true hope I am talking about because of the expectation of your hope being fulfilled. But one definition of hope takes it a step further: "to expect with confidence."[3] This is more the kind of hope I am talking about. You don't just expect your hope to be fulfilled; you confidently expect it to be fulfilled.

The Bible tells us, "Blessed is the man who trusts in the LORD, and whose hope is the LORD" (Jer. 17:7, NKJV).

The Hebrew word for hope in that verse means refuge, confidence, security, and trust. It means a "sure and firm hope."[4] It comes from a root word that means to set your hope and confidence upon someone, to be secure, to be bold, and to fear nothing.[5] That is the kind of hope you can have in Jesus. He is your refuge, He is your confidence, He is your security, and you can trust Him. He is your sure and firm hope. With Jesus as your source of true hope, you can be bold and courageous because there is nothing to fear.

"God is our refuge and strength, a very present help in trouble" (Ps. 46:1).

"The LORD will be your confidence" (Prov. 3:26).

"[God] set my feet upon a rock, making my steps secure" (Ps. 40:2).

"Be strong and courageous. Do not be frightened, and do not be dismayed, for the LORD your God is with you wherever you go" (Josh. 1:9).

"Since we have such a hope, we are very bold" (2 Cor. 3:12).

"So we can confidently say, 'The Lord is my helper; I will not fear'" (Heb. 13:6).

You may be feeling as if you have lost all hope. You may be feeling as if you are dried up, washed up, destroyed, or cut off. But there is hope for you.

In the Book of Ezekiel, the Spirit of the Lord brought the prophet to a valley filled with dead, dry bones. The Lord told Ezekiel that the bones were saying, "Our bones are dried up, and our hope is lost; we are indeed cut off" (Ezek. 37:11). But with God, dead, dry bones don't have to stay that way. God is a God of hope, healing, restoration, and redemption, and with God, nothing is impossible (Luke 1:37). He gives new life to things that are dead. And that is just what He did. Ezekiel prophesied to the bones, just as the Lord commanded him, and the bones were put together with flesh and muscle. Then, the breath of life entered them, and they lived. God said, "I will put my Spirit within you, and you shall live" (Ezek. 37:14).

It's like that with us. When we are dead in our sin, lacking the mercy, grace, and forgiveness we need to be in right relationship with our Creator, we are like dried-up, lifeless bones that have no true hope. But God doesn't want us to stay like that. He sent His Son, Jesus, to die on the cross for our sins so we could have the mercy, grace, and forgiveness we need to be in right relationship with Him. When you give your life to Christ, when you ask Him to forgive you and to come make a home in your heart, it is like dead bones coming to life! Hope is restored! You are born again! You become a new creation in Christ, and all the old junk from your past is washed away, and all things become new. And if that weren't enough, He sends His Holy Spirit to dwell in you, to be your Helper, your Comforter, and your Guide. He gives you new life! And that life is abundant, full of true hope, a hope that the Bible calls "living hope" (1 Pet. 1:3).

The hope that dwells in you because of Jesus isn't like the hope you have for a pony for your birthday when you are six years old. It is a confident expectation that "He who promised is faithful" (Heb. 10:23) and that "He who has begun a good work in you will complete it" (Phil. 1:6). It is living hope because the hope is a person: Jesus.

If you have never put your faith in Jesus Christ as your Lord and Savior, my prayer is that you will do so right now. Don't wait. The Bible says that "now is the day of salvation" (2 Cor. 6:2). All you have to do is believe in your heart and then talk to God, the same way you would talk to a friend. Tell Him that you believe that Jesus died for your sins and was raised from the dead, and ask Him to forgive you. The words don't matter; you can just say what is in your heart. But if you need some help getting started, you can use this prayer:

> Lord Jesus, I believe that You came to the earth to die for my sins. Thank You for loving me so much. Please forgive me of all my sins. Give me new life, and fill me with Your living hope. I trust You as my Lord and Savior. Help me to live my life to bring glory to You. In Jesus' name I pray, Amen.

If you prayed that prayer, let me be the first to welcome you to the family of God. We are far from perfect, but we are family nonetheless, and I am glad you are a part of it. Whether you've just prayed that prayer for the first time, or your still unsure and would like to learn more about Jesus before you do, there is a resource that I believe does a wonderful job introducing you to Jesus. Go to https://joycemeyer.org/study/how-to-know-jesus and learn all about how Jesus and His love and grace can change your life.[1]

How to Keep Pressing Forward in Difficult Times

Even when you have trusted Jesus and asked Him to be your Lord and Savior, you are still going to face difficult times. Jesus actually told us we would have problems: "In this world you will have trouble." But Jesus didn't leave it there. He also said, "But take heart! I have overcome the world" (John 16:33, NIV).

The Bible also says this about the challenges we all face,, "We can rejoice, too, when we run into problems and trials, for we know that they help us develop endurance. And endurance develops strength of character, and character strengthens our confident hope of salvation. And this hope will not lead to disappointment.

For we know how dearly God loves us, because he has given us the Holy Spirit to fill our hearts with his love" (Rom. 5:3-5, NLT).

I know—rejoicing in your problems and trials is easier said than done. However, I have developed some habits over the years that help me keep moving forward, even when times are tough. They help me stay focused on God. They help me triumph over the enemy by renewing my strength so I can keep running the race God has set before me. (I may not be able to physically run, but I'm still running on the inside!)

These five daily habits have helped me grow and keep hold of the hope that I have in Jesus. I know they can help you too.

1. Focus on God when you wake up.

Start your day with the Lord. In the good times, the bad times, and all the in-between times, spending time in His presence is the best way to start your day. You may be going through a situation that is painful and feels hopeless. But even though it may not seem like it, God is with you during the difficult times. His Word promises that He will never leave you or forsake you (Heb. 13:5). He also promised that He will never forget you (Isa. 49:15), so don't forget about Him!

Rather than starting your day by checking your social media accounts or seeing what the news has to say, take some time at the beginning of each day to talk to God. Thank Him for the day, and ask Him to help guide you through it. Praise Him, love Him, and spend a little time with Him. It doesn't have to be elaborate or formal. Talk to Him while you are in the shower or while you are doing your hair. Talk to Him while you're driving to work or school. Make time to spend time with Jesus. It will get your mind and heart ready to face the day, regardless of what the day brings.

And don't just talk to Jesus. Let Him talk to you, too. When you are praying, take time to listen to what the Holy Spirit has to say to you. And let God speak to you through His Word as well. Even if it is just a verse or two, starting your day by reading the Word of God will motivate you, uplift you, and set the focus for your day.

2. Be thankful.

It doesn't matter what kind of situation you are facing; having a thankful heart strengthens you. First Thessalonians 5:18 says, "Give thanks in all circumstances; for this is the will of God in Christ Jesus for you" (emphasis added). There is always something to be thankful for. I may no longer be able to physically move, but I am thankful I still have a sharp mind. I am thankful for a motorized wheelchair that I can drive myself, as well as the computer laser that allows me to control my computer. I am thankful for my family and my friends. I am thankful for my health and for many other blessings.

There may be times when you find it difficult to be thankful. It happens to everyone, including me. But the Bible talks about that, too. Psalm 50:14 says, "Offer to God a sacrifice of thanksgiving." Sometimes, being thankful requires a sacrifice—a sacrifice of yourself. Even when you are in the midst of the storms of life, you always have something to be thankful for. If you have received the gift of salvation from Jesus Christ and will have an eternal home in heaven, you have something to be thankful for. If you have people who love you (even though it may not always feel like it), you have something to be thankful for. If you have the Holy Spirit living inside you, you have something to be thankful for. If you are breathing, you have something to be thankful for.

Every day, think of at least five things for which you are thankful and then thank God for them. "Every good gift and every perfect gift is from above, coming down from the Father of lights"

(Jas. 1:17). As you continue to practice being thankful, your list of things to be thankful for will continue to grow and evolve, and you will continue to grow too. And the more you practice being thankful—for the big things and the small things—the easier it will be to have a grateful heart in challenging circumstances. And being thankful brings another gift along with it: joy. A thankful heart is a joyful heart.

> *Even when you are in the midst of the storms of life, you always have something to be thankful for.*

3. Focus on the positive.

Bad things happen to everyone, and it's easy to focus only on the negative things when they occur. But when you focus on the negative, you are setting yourself up for failure. When your mind is set on the negative, all you will see and get in return is negative because that's where your focus is. Proverbs 23:7 (NKJV) says, "For as he thinks in his heart, so is he," meaning you are what you think. Your thoughts are powerful, which is why you need to take every thought captive to the obedience of Christ (2 Cor. 10:5). Don't let lies, fear, doubt, or worry consume you. Instead, find the positive in every circumstance.

It may take some time to develop this habit, especially if you have been thinking negatively for a long time. But that's OK. Be patient, and keep working at it. You can develop a new habit by replacing the negative thoughts with positive ones. You might start by memorizing a simple Bible verse to help redirect your focus whenever the negative thoughts start creeping in. Psalm 118:24 (NKJV) might be a good place to start, "This is the day the LORD has made; we will rejoice and be glad in it."

A simple tool such as repeating a truth from the word of God can have amazing effects on your perspective. Positive people have a different outlook on life. When you choose to think about good things, the bad things can't take up the space in your mind anymore. Set your mind on the positive instead of the negative, and see how it changes you.

4. Don't let your feelings control you.

Feelings are fickle. Emotions can lead you down dark paths, but you can choose not to let them control your mind. People often ask me, "How do you feel about being paralyzed?" Honestly, some days I feel great about it, and some days I feel sad or upset. However, I have learned a lesson over the years. On one of my negative days, I don't focus on my emotions. I've discovered that if I don't allow my feelings to determine the path of my day, then I can move forward with a more positive outlook and have a blessed day. I can choose to rejoice and be glad in the day the Lord has made for me.

I may not be able to control my circumstances, but I can control how I respond to them. I know it can be hard, but with practice, you can choose to look beyond your feelings. Focus on uplifting thoughts that are more cheerful and positive. When you continually do this, your whole outlook will change. But you have to choose. Not letting your emotions control you goes hand in hand with focusing on the positive. So, choose not to let your emotions control you and choose to focus on the positive—in other words, choose life and blessing.

"I have set before you life and death, blessing and curse. Therefore choose life" (Deut. 30:19).

5. Laugh.

Make it a point to laugh and find joy every d

"A happy heart is good medicine and a ch
healing, but a broken spirit dries up the bc
AMPC).

Laughter relieves stress and lifts up your spirit—free of charge. Take a moment to look beyond your circumstances and laugh out loud; it will refresh your soul. Laughter is proven to make you feel better and disperse worry. If you are having trouble finding something to laugh about, watch a funny movie, listen to a comedian, or watch a couple of YouTube videos of funny kids or animals. God gave us the ability to laugh for a reason. It is a gift from God that brings us joy from the inside out. Let the joy of the Lord comfort you and bring you peace through laughter. The Bible says there is "a time to laugh" (Eccles. 3:4). Find that time every day, for "the joy of the LORD is your strength" (Neh. 8:10).

These five simple habits can help you walk in triumph. While times of struggle can be discouraging, the good news is that we know how the story ends: we win! Victory is ours because of Jesus. I quoted a Bible verse at the beginning of the chapter that bears repeating now, "Now thanks be to God who always leads us in triumph in Christ, and through us diffuses the fragrance of His knowledge in every place" (2 Cor. 2:14).

God has not called you to walk in defeat. He leads you in triumph. In Him, you are more than a conqueror. The five simple habits, focusing on words of life, and especially having the true hope found only in Jesus Christ—these are all things that can help you gain victory in your life. You don't have to let the challenging circumstances in life or the lies of the enemy make you quit. Your faith in God will enable you to overcome and gain victory in any situation. It is a promise you can stand on, "For everyone who has born of God overcomes the world. And this is the victory that as overcome the world—our faith" (I John 5:4).

CHAPTER SEVEN

Divine Healing

I believe I will be healed.

Even from the beginning, when they first told me I was paralyzed from the shoulders down and would be that way for the rest of my life, I never believed it was forever. I believed that I would be healed someday. And to be clear, I am not in denial about my condition and its severity. I am also not looking for medical breakthroughs to heal me. God told me He is going to heal me, and I believe Him. When I am healed, it will be undeniably supernatural. I am not placing my hope in stem cells from aborted babies (I would never agree to a treatment like that; all lives are precious) or an advanced electrical technique, such as functional electrical stimulation, or any other form of medical miracle. I am placing my hope in God alone to heal me.

About fifteen years ago or so, I had a stomach ulcer. It was bleeding and causing all kinds of problems. The treatment I had didn't work, so I was going to have to have yet another surgery to deal with the ulcer. Surgery is, of course, never easy for me, so my mom prayed the end of Psalm 91 over me, changing the pronouns to feminine ones so it was just for me.

Because [she] holds fast to me in love, I will deliver [her]; I will protect [her], because [she] knows my name. When [she] calls to me, I will answer [her]; I will be with [her] in trouble; I will rescue [her] and honor [her]. With long life I will satisfy [her] and show [her] my salvation. (Ps. 91:14–16)

About thirty minutes after my mom prayed for me, they took an X-ray in preparation for my surgery. The X-ray revealed that the ulcer was completely gone. It had disappeared, and surgery was no longer needed. God was with me in my trouble and delivered me from my ulcer. He healed my ulcer then, and I have no doubt that He will heal me completely one day.

What God Has Shown Me

When you are paralyzed, your prognosis is very discouraging. The thought of being confined to a wheelchair for your entire life can be overwhelming. But I wasn't discouraged or overwhelmed because, from the very beginning, I had a deep inner peace about my condition. It was as if God was whispering in my ear all along, "This is not forever."

Inner peace can be a great indicator of God's will at work in your life. While not foolproof (sometimes our own will gets the best of us), whenever I am making a big decision, whether I have that sense of inner peace can tell me if I am following the will of God for my life or if I am letting my own will, my own wants, and my own wishes get in the way. And because I have had peace in my heart about being healed for so long, I know without a doubt that it is God's will for me to be healed.

I also believe that the ultimate purpose of my paralysis is to glorify God. That being said, it also means that my healing will be perfectly timed to bring the most glory to God.

As I wait for God to heal me, I sometimes think about the story of the woman with the issue of blood.

"There was a woman who had had a discharge of blood for twelve years, and who had suffered much under many physicians, and had spent all that she had, and was no better but rather grew worse. She had heard the reports about Jesus and came up behind him in the crowd and touched his garment. For she said, 'If I touch even his garments, I will be made well.' And immediately the flow of blood dried up, and she felt in her body that she was healed of her disease. And Jesus, perceiving in himself that power had gone out from him, immediately turned about in the crowd and said, 'Who touched my garments?' And his disciples said to him, 'You see the crowd pressing around you, and yet you say, 'Who touched me?'" And he looked around to see who had done it. But the woman, knowing what had happened to her, came in fear and trembling and fell down before him and told him the whole truth. And he said to her, 'Daughter, your faith has made you well; go in peace, and be healed of your disease'" (Mark 5:25-34)

The issue of blood was definitely an issue for this woman. It made her unclean in the eyes of the Law, meaning that she would not have been allowed in the temple for Jewish holidays and ceremonies. In addition, anyone or anything she touched would have also become ceremonially unclean. Can you imagine spending twelve years with everyone, including the people you love, avoiding touching you so they wouldn't become unclean? Can you imagine trying to provide for your daily needs when everything you touched was then considered unclean? Even going to the market to buy food would be nearly impossible since no one would want to brush up against you in the crowded streets and merchants would not want you to touch their products.

Twelve years is a long time to deal with a physical ailment. Trust me, I have this woman beat by quite a few years, and I can relate to how she must have been feeling. She had tried every possible earthly solution, but nothing worked. In fact, she got worse. (There's a lesson in there about seeking earthly solutions before seeking heavenly ones.) But then she started hearing stories about a man named Jesus, who calmed storms, cast out demons, and taught the truth in a way no one had ever heard before. He also healed—fevers, leprosy, paralysis, a withered hand, and other illnesses and ailments. And I believe that when the woman heard these things, she recognized that Jesus was the long-awaited Messiah, and she was also reminded of a prophecy about the Messiah, "The Sun of Righteousness shall arise with healing in His wings" (Malachi 4:2).

The Hebrew word for wings in that verse is kānāpi. While it does mean wings, it can also mean edge, border, or the corner of a garment.[1] It is the same word used in the Book of Numbers when the Lord gives instructions about the children of Israel making fringes on the borders of their garments to remind them of the commandments of the Lord (15:38-40). It is the reason the tallit, or Jewish prayer shawl, has fringes on the border. As a Jewish man, Jesus would have worn a tallit.

That is why the woman said, "If I touch even his garments, I will be made well" (Mark 5:28). She recognized Jesus as the Sun of Righteousness, and she had the faith to believe that touching His wings, the border of His tallit, would result in the healing she so desperately needed. And so, at great risk, since she was considered unclean, she worked her way through the crowds around Jesus. And just as was prophe-

> *I am not afraid to declare with boldness that I have faith that God will heal me.*

sied in the Book of Malachi, the Sun of Righteousness had healing in His wings. The woman was healed.

Her healing was perfectly timed to bring glory to God. The manner of her healing, the simple act of touching the border of Jesus' tallit, fulfilled a prophecy given hundreds of years before. Her knowledge of the Scriptures, her faith, and her boldness all combined to bring her to the perfect moment for her healing. I want the same thing to be said of me.

What Does the Word Say?

I am content to wait on God's timing so that my healing may bring the utmost glory to Him, and I am not afraid to declare with boldness that I have faith that God will heal me. The Scriptures are full of verses about healing, and they help boost my faith whenever the enemy tries to make me think my healing is beyond God's power.

"I am the LORD, your healer" (Ex. 15:26).

"And Jesus answered them, 'Go and tell John what you hear and see: the blind receive their sight and the lame walk, lepers are cleansed and the deaf hear, and the dead are raised up, and the poor have good news preached to them'" (Matt. 11:4-5).

"O LORD my God, I cried to you for help, and you have healed me" (Ps. 30:2).

"Bless the LORD, O my soul, and forget not all his benefits, who forgives all your iniquity, who heals all your diseases, who redeems your life from the pit, who crowns you with steadfast love and mercy, who satisfies you with good so that your youth is renewed like the eagle's" (Ps. 103:2-5).

"He sent out his word and healed them" (Ps. 107:20).

"He heals the brokenhearted and binds up their wounds" (Ps.

147:3).

"But he was pierced for our transgressions; he was crushed for our iniquities; upon him was the chastisement that brought us peace, and with his wounds we are healed" (Is. 53:5).

"So his fame spread throughout all Syria, and they brought him all the sick, those afflicted with various diseases and pains, those oppressed by demons, those having seizures, and paralytics, and he healed them" (Matt. 4:24).

The Gospels are full of stories of people being healed by Jesus, including people who are paralyzed like me. The story of the healing at the pool in Bethesda says that the man Jesus healed had been lame for thirty-eight years and "had already been there a long time" (John 5:6). I can relate to that.

The man had also seen other people being healed whenever the waters of the pool were stirred, but his turn had never come. I don't know how often people were healed at the pool, but it must have been so frustrating to lie there day after day, week after week, month after month, year after year, and perhaps even decade after decade, watching others get the healing he longed for and wondering if it would ever be his turn. I can relate to that, too. I have seen God do miraculous things, and He has even miraculously healed me of certain things—but I am still paralyzed.

The waiting isn't always easy. But I still have faith. I still trust God. I still trust that His plan for me is better than anything I could come up with on my own. I trust that God's Word is true. And I know that one day, in God's perfect timing and in His perfect way, I will walk. I will dance. I will throw my arms around the people I love and hug them the way I haven't been able to for decades. I will be healed.

Prophecies About My Healing

I have never believed that my paralysis was permanent. From the beginning, I knew that God would heal me. And God has brought other people across my path to reinforce that knowledge.

I was in the Walmart parking lot one day about seven years ago when a middle-aged man came up to me and asked if he could pray for me. While he was praying, he started speaking in tongues. When he was finished, he told me, "You are going to be healed." He also shared his testimony that he had been in a wheelchair for five years, but God had healed him, and he was now walking. He also said that while he was praying for me, God showed him that I was going to be healed. It was a powerful confirmation for me.

In addition to that, over the years, I have had many people come up to me and share that they had dreams about my being healed. I believe that God speaks to people in dreams, and I know that some dreams given to people are prophetic. All these dreams that people have shared with me just continue to confirm what I already know in my heart: I will be healed.

The Struggle Is Real

While I know God will heal me, I am still paralyzed. That is not always easy. I won't lie and say that I don't struggle with waiting on God's timing.

Physically, I have been through a lot over the years. A broken neck was just the beginning. I coded a few times due to complications from my injury. I have had surgery multiple times, including, among others, a bladder augmentation, having my gallbladder removed, having a shunt put in my neck to fix a cyst against my spinal cord, a broken hip repair, and a hysterectomy to address problems

> *No physical attack from the enemy, whether big or small, is going to keep me from running my race.*

with endometriosis. I've had autoimmune hemolytic anemia, MRSA, sepsis syndrome, and other significant infections. When you write it all down, it looks like quite an overwhelming list, but God carried me through it all.

My mom actually calls me Timex sometimes because I take a licking and keep on ticking. I am not going to let any of the physical challenges I face hold me back from fulfilling my God-given purpose. Satan may think he has me right where he wants me, but I know better. I know that I am still here for a purpose, and I want to glorify God through that purpose. And so no physical attack from the enemy, whether big or small, is going to keep me from running my race. (I know, I know; I can't run. But as I have said before, I am still running on the inside.)

I know without a doubt that God has been there with me every step of the way, healing me of various things and getting me help right when I needed it through all of it. He has continued to direct my path, and I will continue to follow where He leads.

I'm not saying it is easy, though. Physical pain is exactly that—a pain! Sometimes it gets to me. For example, a few years back, something fell on my chair and bent the frame, affecting the headrest. It caused extreme pain to run through the back of my head on a regular basis. For one of the few places I can 100 percent feel on my body, to be in constant pain causes torment. While changing the position of my head does help, if I move ever so slightly, the pain penetrates my head again. I also have a lot of back pain from the thinning of the discs in my back, arthritis, and scoliosis from my body position all these years.

I used to feel as if admitting I was hurting, whether physically or emotionally, was a sign of weakness. "Just ignore it," I would say to myself and pretend everything was just fine. But pretending only puts a bandage over it, hiding it without allowing space for healing physically and emotionally. Being open with God about your pain is a good place to start on the road to healing. When I am in pain, I can reach deep inside to find God's strength to press through and also to find words to encourage others in the process.

When people think about healing, they typically think about physical healing, but the reality is that we need emotional heal-

> *Jesus came to heal the brokenhearted, those who are bound by emotional wounds, those who mourn, those who are weighed down by the cares of this world, and those who are burdened by shame. And He came to give them everlasting joy.*

ing, too. We have deep emotional wounds and scars that we are walking around with, but the truth is that God wants to heal those things, too. The Word says that Jesus healed "all kinds" of things.

"And Jesus went about all Galilee, teaching in their synagogues, preaching the gospel of the kingdom, and healing all kinds of sickness and all kinds of disease among the people" (Matt. 4:23, NKJV).

Emotional pain can be just as limiting as physical pain. But God's healing is just as much available for emotional hurts as it is for physical ones. There is a beautiful prophecy about Jesus in the Old Testament.

> The Spirit of the Lord GOD is upon me, because the LORD has anointed me to bring good news to the poor; he has sent me to bind up the brokenhearted, to proclaim liberty to the captives, and the opening of the prison to those who are bound; to proclaim the year of the LORD's favor, and the day of vengeance of our God; to comfort all who mourn; to grant to those who mourn in Zion—to give them a beautiful headdress instead of ashes, the oil of gladness instead of mourning, the garment of praise instead of a faint spirit; that they may be called oaks of righteousness, the planting of the LORD, that he may be glorified....Instead of your shame there shall be a double portion; instead of dishonor they shall rejoice in their lot; therefore in their land they shall possess a double portion; they shall have everlasting joy. (Is. 61:1-3, 7)

When Jesus walked the earth, He read a portion of this passage aloud in the synagogue and said, "Today this Scripture has been fulfilled in your hearing" (Luke 4:21). Jesus came to heal the brokenhearted, those who are bound by emotional wounds, those who mourn, those who are weighed down by the cares of this world, and those who are burdened by shame. And He came to give them everlasting joy.

I have struggled with frustration and disappointment as I wait to be healed. And I know there are lots of people out there who are hurting way more than I am and in many different areas. But I also know that we serve a God who heals. It is even one of His names: "the LORD who heals you" (Exod. 15:26, NKJV). God has a purpose for my life, and He has a purpose for your life. While the pain is never easy, I know that God will work it out for my good and for yours. His Word promises that, "And we know that for those who love God all things work together for good, for those who are called according to his purpose" (Rom. 8:28).

I know that the waiting time is something people can struggle with physically, emotionally, and spiritually, and while I am far from perfect in that area and I definitely had some issues, my waiting time taught me to put my trust wholly and completely in God. Have I been disappointed that the wait has been so long? Absolutely. But I am still going to choose to trust God for His timing. "But I trust in you, O LORD; I say, "You are my God." My times are in your hand" (Ps. 31:14-15).

The fact that it has been so long and I'm still not healed doesn't mean it is not God's will for me to be healed. God can and will free me from this paralysis any minute, but until it happens, I will continue to live life, looking beyond my circumstances and knowing He is with me every step of the way. And I will be healed.

CHAPTER EIGHT

Biding Time

It's hard to believe it has been twenty-nine years. I have been in a chair almost twice as long as I was up and walking around. When you really stop and think about it, twenty-nine years is a long time. But during the waiting time, God has been showing me so many things and teaching me to trust Him. Because I have learned not to let my emotions control me and to keep my mind focused on God's plan and bringing glory to Him through my life, it has made the waiting time easier. Being healed just because I want to be healed right now wouldn't necessarily bring the most glory to God. By keeping my perspective right, I can continue to wait patiently, knowing that God will bring about my healing at the perfect time for Him to receive the maximum amount of glory, for He is the one who deserves all the glory and all the praise.

As I have said, I knew I was going to be healed from the very beginning, and my paralysis was not going to be permanent. Worrying about being healed and its timing wasn't something that even crossed my mind during the first few years. I was secure in the knowledge that God would heal me in His timing, and in the meantime, I had plenty to think about with just learning how to live life as a quadriplegic.

What It Means to Wait

We all go through different seasons in life. The Word of God says there is a season for everything:

> For everything there is a season, and a time for every matter under heaven: a time to be born, and a time to die; a time to plant, and a time to pluck up what is planted; a time to kill, and a time to heal; a time to break down, and a time to build up; a time to weep, and a time to laugh; a time to mourn, and a time to dance. (Eccl. 3:1-4)

I am in a waiting season. While I continue living my life and striving every day to do the things God has called me to do, I am still waiting. I am waiting for the time when the Lord will rescue me from my paralysis. I am expectantly waiting for the due season when He will open His hand and show me favor by completely healing my body so I can walk again.

"I stand silently before the Lord, waiting for him to rescue me. For salvation comes from him alone. Yes, he alone is my Rock, my rescuer, defense and fortress. Why then should I be tense with fear when troubles come?" (Ps. 62:1-2, TLB).

"The eyes of all wait for You [looking, watching, and expecting] and You give them their food in due season. You open Your hand and satisfy every living thing with favor" (Ps. 145:15-16, AMPC).

During this season of waiting, this season of biding time until my healing is made manifest, I have to know what is true. I have to know in my mind and in my heart what the Word says so when the enemy attacks me with his lies, I can wield the sword of the Spirit and destroy the lies before they have a chance to take root. I need to be rooted and grounded in the Word of God so that when my season comes, I bear the fruit God intends for me.

Blessed is the man who walks not in the counsel of the wicked, nor stands in the way of sinners, nor sits in the seat of scoffers; but his delight is in the law of the LORD, and on his law he meditates day and night. He is like a tree planted by streams of water that yields its fruit in its season.

When I stay focused on the Word, when I meditate on it and write it on my heart, it helps my roots grow down deep. The Word of God is like seeds of truth that have been planted deep in my heart, and I must continue to cultivate them so they grow and produce fruit. Just because I am in a waiting season doesn't mean it can't also be a growing season.

As I mentioned in the last chapter, the Bible is full of stories of the power of God to heal. When Jesus walked the earth, He healed numerous people. One of God's names is the Lord your Healer (Exod. 15:26). And the Word also says, "God is no respecter of persons" (Acts 10:34, MEV). Since God doesn't show partiality and He has healed others, that means He will heal me— and He will also heal you. You may think that is impossible, but the truth is that "nothing is impossible with God (Luke 1:37). And as Joyce Meyer puts it, "As children of God, one of the privileges we have is believing the impossible."[1]

I know that God's Word is living, active, and true. And His Word says that I am already healed. "By his wounds we are healed" (Is. 53:5).

It doesn't say that we were healed by His wounds, as if it were a one-time thing that happened at the moment we got saved or something like that. And it doesn't say we will be healed as if it is a promise that will only come true when we get to heaven. The Word says that we are healed. It is in the present tense, meaning it is for now rather than in the past or in the future. Since God's Word is true, I am already healed. I am just waiting for that healing to manifest.

You may be waiting on God to heal you, too, whether you need physical healing, emotional healing, spiritual healing, or maybe even all three. But what does it really mean to wait on God?

One of the most well-known verses on waiting is Isaiah 40:31, "They who wait for the LORD shall renew their strength; they shall mount up with wings like eagles; they shall run and not be weary; they shall walk and not faint.

That is an amazing promise from God. When we wait on Him, we will have our strength renewed. We will not be weary in the face of challenges or faint in the face of struggles. Waiting on God can make you feel like an eagle, soaring through the sky with the whole world stretched out before you—no limits and no fear. Waiting on the Lord definitely has some benefits.

The word *wait*, of course, can mean to be in expectation of something, like waiting for something to happen. And when we wait in expectation of what God is going to do and don't try to make things happen ourselves, it serves to strengthen us. But wait can also mean to serve, like someone waiting on you in a restau-

> *If you and God are like loose strands, you are not going to get much strength from the relationship. But if you are closely bound to the Lord, you will have all the strength you need during the waiting time.*

rant. It is also true that when we serve the Lord, it strengthens us and develops our character. But the Hebrew meaning of the word *wait* goes a little deeper.

The Hebrew word used in Isaiah 40:31 is qāvâ. It means "to bind together." It has the sense of twisting together strands of rope to make it stronger.[2] That puts a whole different spin on the verse in Isaiah: those who are bound together with the Lord will renew their strength, mount up with wings like eagles, and run and not be weary.

Think of a piece of rope. If the strands are loose and not bound together tightly, it is not very strong. The rope gets its strength from the fibers being tightly bound together. The same is true in regard to your relationship with God. If you and God are like loose strands, you are not going to get much strength from the relationship. But if you are closely bound to the Lord, you will have all the strength you need during the waiting time.

I have seen the evidence of this in my own life. During my waiting time, I have been seeking the Lord. I have been reading His Word, spending time in prayer with Him, and worshipping the God I love. My relationship with Him has grown stronger and stronger over the years, and He is my strength, my rock, my fortress, and my deliverer. My relationship with Him, being bound together with Him, has given me both the strength and the inner peace to go through my waiting time with patience and perseverance, knowing that God is in control, His plan for me is good, and His timing is perfect.

Encouragement from the Word

Isaiah 40:31 has been a really important verse to me during my journey. It encourages me and reminds me that I do not need to grow weary during the waiting time. I know that God will continue to strengthen me and renew me until the day when I once again will walk and run and dance! I also know that if I weren't trusting His Word, believing that His promises are true, and staying grounded in my relationship with Him, I would grow weary. I want to be "like a tree planted by streams of water that yields its fruit in its season" (Ps. 1:3), and I can't do that if I am not grounded in the Word.

The Word of God is a constant source of encouragement to me. When I am feeling down or discouraged during my waiting season, I turn to the Bible. It is full of powerful reminders of things I know to be true. So, when I feel weak, I can be reminded of where my strength comes from.

"'My grace is sufficient for you, for my power is made perfect in weakness.' Therefore I will boast all the more gladly of my weaknesses, so that the power of Christ may rest upon me. For the sake of Christ, then, I am content with weaknesses, insults, hardships, persecutions, and calamities. For when I am weak, then I am strong" (2 Cor. 12:9-10).

"The joy of the Lord is your strength: (Neh. 8:10).

When I feel discouraged, I can be reminded of the true source of hope.

"And now, O Lord, for what do I wait? My hope is in you" (Ps. 39:7).

"Why are you cast down, O my soul, and why are you in turmoil within me? Hope in God; for I shall again praise him, my salvation and my God" (Ps. 42:11).

"You are my hiding place and my shield; I hope in your word" (Ps. 119:114).

> That the God of our Lord Jesus Christ, the Father of glory, may give you the Spirit of wisdom and of revelation in the knowledge of him, having the eyes of your

hearts enlightened, that you may know what is the hope to which he has called you, what are the riches of his glorious inheritance in the saints, and what is the immeasurable greatness of his power toward us who believe. (Eph. 1:17-19)

Whatever I am feeling, whatever I am struggling with, whatever is getting me down while I am biding time until my season of complete physical healing—God's Word has something to say about it. And because I know that "all the promises of God in Him are Yes, and in Him Amen, to the glory of God through us" (2 Cor. 1:20, NKJV), I am not just reading empty words. I am reading promises that I know will be fulfilled in my life to the glory of God.

There are lots of inspiring words out there. You can go to one of the innumerable quote websites out there and find all kinds of sayings that encourage you, inspire you, and challenge you. And a lot of the sayings are true or at least partially true. But they are not the truth. Jesus said, "I am the way, and the truth, and the life" (John 14:6). He also prayed for you and me in the Garden of Gethsemane right before He arrested, saying, "Sanctify them in the truth; your word is truth" (John 17:17).

When you are in a waiting season, you need to make sure you are reading the truth, the living, active Word of God. Don't get me wrong—you can read other things. I read all kinds of books, articles, and blogs from lots of different authors, and I have read many things that have encouraged, inspired, and challenged me. But to really

> *No matter the circumstances, no matter how long the wait, God is worthy of our praise.*

nourish the seeds of truth that have been planted in your heart, to really be able to defend against the fiery darts of the enemy, to really grow and flourish and triumph over defeat in your waiting season, you need the Word of God.

You need to read it, hear it, speak it, memorize it, and write it on the tablet of your heart— because the words in the Word are the only ones with the full power of the Lord God Almighty behind them.

Worship While You Wait

On the wall in my kitchen, I have a picture that says, "Until God opens the next door, praise Him in the hallway." And that needs to be the attitude of hearts while we are waiting. No matter the circumstances, no matter how long the wait, God is worthy of our praise.

Psalm 3:3 says, "You, O LORD, are a shield about me, my glory, and the lifter of my head." You may be feeling depressed, dismayed, down in the dumps, or discouraged during your waiting season, but God is waiting to lift your head. So spend time with Him, worshipping and praising the Lord who loves you beyond what you could ever imagine.

Make a joyful noise to the LORD, all the earth! Serve the LORD with gladness! Come into his presence with singing! Know that the LORD, he is God! It is he who made us, and we are his; we are his people, and the sheep of his pasture. Enter his gates with thanksgiving, and his courts with praise! Give thanks to him; bless his name! For the LORD is good; his steadfast love endures forever, and his faithfulness to all generations. (Ps. 100:1-5)

Do you know what is amazing about when God lifts your head like a loving Father lifting the head of His precious son or daughter who is struggling or brokenhearted? When you lift your eyes, you can see where your help is coming from.

I lift up my eyes to the hills. From where does my help come? My help comes from the LORD, who made heaven and earth.

You may not understand why you are facing a particular struggle, and you may not know when God is going to open the next door so your waiting can come to an end. But that doesn't change the fact that God's promises are true. He has a plan for you, and that plan is good. He causes all things to work together for your good. With Him, all things are possible. He sees you, He knows you, and He calls you by name. And there is nothing too hard for Him. So keep praising Him, and wait in faith that His Word will be fulfilled in your life.

There is someone in the Bible who knew a lot about waiting: Joseph. When Joseph was only seventeen years old, God gave him some dreams that showed his parents and brothers bowing down to him. When he shared these dreams with his family, it did not go very well. Long story short: his brothers sold him into slavery and told his father he was dead; he was put in charge of his master's house, but his master's wife lied and said he tried to rape her, so he went to prison and he got put in charge of the prisoners; he helped a prisoner by correctly interpreting his dream, but the prisoner forgot about him when he got out. Joseph definitely had a rough time in Egypt. Joseph spent thirteen years as a slave or in prison. But even after his time as a slave and prisoner ended and he became overseer of all Egypt, second only to Pharaoh, the dreams God gave him were still not fulfilled. He was still in a waiting season. God had opened a door for him, but it was not the door he had been waiting on for so long. God positioned him to save many lives during a seven-year famine using his God-given wisdom and insight, but his

> *He sees you, He knows you, and He calls you by name. And there is nothing too hard for Him.*

dreams were yet to come to pass. He knew what God had shown him, but he had yet to see it fulfilled.

But Joseph remained faithful to the Lord throughout all his trials. His waiting season— both the time as a slave and a prisoner and the time in a position of authority—didn't cause him to lose sight of God. He trusted that God was behind everything that had happened to him. He trusted God's plan for his life. His heart to still worship the Lord in his waiting season was revealed in the names he chose for his sons, both of whom were born during that waiting season. He named his first son Manasseh, which means "causing to forget,"[3] saying, "God has made me forget all my hardship" (Gen. 41:51). He named his second son Ephraim, which means "I shall be doubly fruitful,"[4] saying, "God has made me fruitful in the land of my affliction" (v. 52). The names of Joseph's sons acknowledged the hardship and affliction Joseph had experienced. He didn't pretend like his trials never happened. But the names of Joseph's sons also acknowledged that Joseph knew he served a good God, who hadn't forgotten him, who hadn't abandoned him, and who had been working everything for his good, even when it was hard, and it seemed as if his trials would never end.

Despite a lengthy waiting season, which was actually still ongoing, Joseph knew that God was worthy of praise. And he acknowledged the goodness of God in an act of worship by naming his sons as he did. Joseph's waiting season didn't end until he was thirty-nine years old, twenty-two long years after his brothers had sold him into slavery. Joseph's father, Jacob, had sent ten of his eleven brothers to Egypt in search of food during a famine. Joseph's brothers ended up bowing down to him as the overseer of Egypt, just as Joseph's dream had foretold, even though his brothers had yet to recognize who Joseph really was. Joseph's wait for the fulfillment of what God had shown him was finally over. In the moment that he revealed his identity to his brothers, he told them, "God sent me before you to preserve for you a remnant on earth and to keep alive for you many survivors. So it was not you who sent me here, but God" (Gen 45:7-8). God had a purpose for all that Joseph went through, positioning him to be able to save what was likely tens of thousands if not hundreds of thousands of lives, including those of his father and his brothers and their families. And when Joseph's waiting season finally ended, God got all the glory.

In my own life, just like in Joseph's life, I have seen God open doors, even though I am still waiting to be healed. In the aftermath of my accident, one of the issues we were facing was the astronomical amount of expenses involved in my care. While I had insurance, the insurance would eventually run out. But equipment, medical procedures, caregivers, and countless other things that I needed and would need in the future all cost a lot of money. Whether there would be sufficient money for my care was a huge determining factor in my quality of life going forward.

There were multiple factors that contributed to my accident and the severity of my injury. First, the seatbelt in the vehicle was faulty. It was one of those seatbelts that had the crosspiece and the lap belt separate. The crosspiece automatically went into place when you shut the door, but you still had to buckle the lap belt. When we got in the wreck, the crosspiece functioned properly and tightened, but the lap belt loosened, allowing my hips to slide forward and causing the other part of the seatbelt to break my neck.

Second, the county had had orders to repair the road where the accident happened for several months because of the number of accidents that had occurred there. However, it still had not been repaired.

In addition, the shopping center next to the accident location had a retaining wall that was supposed to prevent runoff from the parking lot from flooding into the street. However, the wall had fallen into disrepair, allowing large amounts of water to flood the street.

> *Exercise that faith muscle, believe that God not only can but that He will, and watch your faith grow into one that truly believes that with God all things are possible.*

All three of these things contributed to the accident and my injuries. We sought financial reimbursement from all three entities: the vehicle manufacturer, the county, and the shopping center. We were able to settle out of court with the vehicle manufacturer and the county, but we had to go to court with the shopping center. However, the outcome was that I was provided with sufficient funds to cover all my medical care and other needs.

My mom was freaking out while all this was going on. She was so worried about how we would pay for my care. But I kept telling her not to worry. God had given me peace that everything would be taken care of. And it was. However, it took five years for everything with the money to get worked out. I knew God was going to provide—His Word promises as much— but I still had to wait on His timing. But I didn't let the wait keep me from worshipping. And I will not let waiting for my healing keep me from worshipping either. God has been so good to me, and nothing is going to stop me from giving Him the praise He deserves.

During the waiting time, there may be times when you feel as if either God isn't hearing you or you aren't hearing Him, especially when your circumstances aren't changing. But God's Word promises that He hears us when we call, and it also promises that because of Jesus' work on the cross, we have access to the throne of grace to find help in times of trouble. So, don't get discouraged, and don't stop praying and seeking God's will and His hand at work in your life. If you are struggling to believe Him for the big things, start believing Him for the small things. Remember, your faith is like a muscle. The more you exercise it, the stronger it will grow. So, if you are struggling to believe God can provide the funds for you to catch up on your mortgage payments when you have been out of work for six months, start by believing He will provide the twenty-five dollars to pay your water bill. And if you are struggling to believe that God can heal your paralysis so you can walk again, start by believing He will heal your headache. Exercise that faith muscle, believe that God not only can but that He will, and watch your faith grow into one that truly believes that with God, all things are possible.

And while you are waiting, stay bound together with the Lord. Keep hoping, keep praying, keep worshipping, and keep finding encouragement in the living Word of God. God always keeps His promises; you can count on it! "Until God opens the next door, praise Him in the hallway."

CHAPTER NINE

The Power of Perspective

Perspective is powerful. How you look at a situation defines and changes how you feel about it. Have you ever noticed that two people can go through the exact same situation together and come out looking at it from two completely different perspectives?

People can perceive things in different ways, it's true. But you can choose how you look at things. Merriam-Webster's first definition of perspective is "a mental view or prospect." That is, of course, true. Perspective is, at its most basic, how you look at things. However, another definition of perspective better captures my idea of it: "the capacity to view things in their true relations or relative importance."[1] Perspective, and keeping a healthy one, is about looking at things as they really are, as part of the bigger picture of your life and God's plan for it, and being able to recognize whether things that happen are really important.

Perspective Matters

Your perspective is closely connected to your attitude. Your attitude can carry you through life with either a positive or a negative outlook. When your outlook on life remains negative, you often get stuck in a holding pattern, unable to move forward. That is what happened to the Israelites.

The Israelites ended up in Egypt because of a famine. As we talked about earlier, God orchestrated the circumstances in Joseph's life to save the lives of thousands of people, including Jacob (who was renamed Israel) and his twelve sons. They were the people of Israel, and in Egypt, "they multiplied and grew exceedingly strong so that the land was filled with them" (Exod. 1:7). Things were great at first because of their connection to Joseph, who was Pharaoh's right-hand man. But then a new ruler came along who did not know Joseph, and because there were so many Israelites by that time, he was worried they would turn against him. So he enslaved them and "made their lives bitter with hard service, in mortar and brick, and in all kinds of work in the field. In all their work, they ruthlessly made them work as slaves" (v. 14).

This went on for years, and "the people of Israel groaned because of their slavery and cried out for help. Their cry for rescue from slavery came up to God. And God heard their groaning, and God remembered his covenant with Abraham, with Isaac, and with Jacob" (Exod. 2:23-24). So, God rescued the Israelites from their slavery in Egypt. He used Moses, Aaron, some plagues, and some mighty miracles to deliver them from their bondage and set them on a journey to the Promised Land, a land flowing with milk and honey.

But they had a perspective problem.

From the moment the Lord brought them out of Egypt, the children of Israel constantly murmured, complained, and voiced their unbelief about God's promise. One of the first issues they complained about was the food. They said, "Would that we had died by the hand of the Lord in the land of Egypt when we sat by the meat pots and ate bread to the full, for you have brought us out into this wilderness to kill this whole assembly with hunger" (Exod. 16:3). Even though God had delivered them from Egypt with an undeniably supernatural series of signs, wonders, and miracles, they doubted God's ability to provide food for them to the point of saying that they would rather be slaves again as long as they had full bellies.

So God provided them with manna, food with the ideal nutritional content for wandering in the wilderness. But they complained about that, too. They complained about water, about waiting for Moses to come back down from Mount Sinai, and about Moses himself.

Their perspective was so skewed that they said they would prefer lives of slavery—lives of bitter service that caused them to groan and cry out for rescue. They had longed to be rescued, but when God rescued them, they didn't allow

> *Don't wander in the wilderness when God has given you the Promised Land.*

gratitude, faith, and hope to color their perspectives. Instead, they chose grumbling, disbelief, and complaining. They kept their eyes on their circumstances instead of on God.

When they finally got to the Promised Land, their perspective was still a problem. Even though God had told them the Promised Land was theirs for the taking, the reports that there were giants in the land caused them to think it would never be theirs. By focusing on the giants instead of God and not keeping a proper perspective of their situation based on the countless daily miracles God had done for them, they missed out on the fulfillment of God's promise. Their attitude toward their circumstances caused them to wander in the wilderness for forty years rather than enter the Promised Land. They were stuck going around the same mountain over and over again for years because they let fear get the best of them.

Don't get stuck going around the same mountain over and over again. Don't wander in the wilderness when God has given you the Promised Land. Don't long for a life of slavery when

God has given you freedom. Fix your perspective. Fix your attitude. Fix your eyes on Jesus. Fix your heart to have faith in His promises and hope in His Word.

My Perspective

I am admittedly a bit of a perfectionist. Some might even say I have OCD. And when you are paralyzed and dependent on other people to do almost everything for you, perfectionism can cause some problems. In the early days after my accident, trying to achieve perfection through the people helping me did not go very well. In fact, it was impossible. I would get mad, aggravated, irritated, and frustrated, and I would allow my emotions to ruin my whole day. I would stress myself out over things like my favorite shirt not being hung up exactly where I wanted it in my closet or my sandwich not being made exactly according to my specifications.

But one day, I thought to myself, "Is it worth all this?" I took time to consider my perspective, and I realized I needed to make a change. The truth is that your perspective can change everything.

It's amazing how when you can't move, your senses go into superwoman mode. Even though I can't always physically see what someone is doing, depending on the position of my chair, I can tell what is going on by the way it sounds. And even though I can't feel most of my body, I can tell what's going on by the pressure being applied. With the combination of my get-up-and-do attitude that I had before my accident, the superwoman senses, and the perfectionism, I often reacted to the way things were being done before I gave things a chance to play out, especially when I first was paralyzed.

But as I considered my situation from a different perspective, I realized that it wasn't worth it to stay stressed out and angry over things not being done exactly the way I wanted them to be. I could choose to stay mad and irritated, or I could choose to change my attitude and change my perspective. I could choose to enjoy life instead of being in a funk because someone didn't hang up my shirt in the "right" spot in the closet.

As I have grown and learned to adapt to different situations, I have let my perfectionism and my emotions get the best of me less and less, but I admit it is still a learning process. There is a fine balance that comes into play. I know that the people who care for me are perfectly capable of fixing a sandwich all by themselves, but I may direct them on how to do it simply because I prefer mine a little differently. . It's nothing personal, and by no means does it suggest that I think they are unable to do things on their own.

And to tell you the truth, when you have to tell someone how you like things 24/7, explaining how you want things done just becomes a habit. Even with the nurses who have been with me for years and years, I still find myself explaining everything. And since different people have different personalities, one wants you to explain how you want things in detail, while someone else would prefer you to say as little as possible. It's hard to swing from one to the other. Truthfully, trying to figure out how much to say or not to say to each person is exhausting. So I just do the best I can do— some days better than others—and move forward the best I know how. And I make sure I keep my perspective right. There are things that are not worth making a big deal over, especially at the expense of the feelings of the people who have been caring for me for years. Each of them has been in my life for a reason, and I'm thankful for them. Gratitude, something the Israelites lacked, is an important part of keeping a correct perspective.

As a quadriplegic trying to find balance in my life, keeping a positive perspective and a positive attitude has made all the difference. Keeping my focus on the Lord and trusting in His plan for my life helps me keep that positive attitude because it gives me hope. Joni Eareckson Tada, who is a quadriplegic just like I am, once wrote, "We desperately need soul-settling hope, the kind of hope that's infinite—never fading and always brightening our darkest paths. We need the hope of God to fill and overflow our hearts, transforming us into people who are confident and at peace with ourselves, our God, and our circumstances."[2]

We all need that infinite, true hope, the kind of hope that is found only in Jesus Christ. You need to have that hope, but if your perspective is skewed and you are always viewing things as negative, it will be really hard to maintain your hope, especially in the face of difficult circumstances. But during difficult times, you need that hope all the more, as well as the peace that comes with it.

My positive perspective has always given me the patience to endure my situation. I know that my accident and my injury were part of God's plan for my life. I know that His plan for me is good. And I know I will be healed. I just need to wait on God's timing.

"He has made everything beautiful in its time" (Eccl. 3:11).

That phrase—*in its time*—is a powerful one. God sees the timeline of all eternity, and I trust that my healing will occur in its time, that is, the perfect time for it to bring the most glory to God. And what a time that will be! The same chapter in Ecclesiastes also says there is "a time to dance" (v. 4). It hasn't been that time for me, at least physically, for a long time, but I am looking forward to the day when it finally is my time to dance again.

So in the meantime, I will just keep trusting God and His eternal perspective on my situation. I will continue to place my hope in Him, for He is my living hope. I will keep a heart of gratitude that allows me to appreciate the small things, the little everyday blessings of my life. I will keep a positive perspective despite my circumstances, for when I do that, it gives me the ability to use my circumstances to glorify God instead of blaming Him.

Making Sure Your Perspective Lines Up with the Word of God

Another vital aspect of maintaining a proper perspective in life is making sure your perspective lines up with the Word of God. I am so thankful we have the Bible. It allows us to know the heart of God, His character, and His voice. It allows us to know the truth, and the truth sets us free.

For example, God is loving and caring, so your perspective needs to line up with that. If you are hearing things that don't coincide with the character of God as revealed in Scripture and through your relationship with Him, those things are not of God. God described Himself to Moses this way, "The LORD, the LORD, a God merciful and gracious, slow to anger, and abounding in steadfast love and faithfulness" (Ex. 34:6).

So, if you look at your circumstances and decide God must be angry with you and punishing you for something, your perspective is not lining up with the Word. God is slow to anger, and He is merciful and gracious. While it is possible that your circumstances are the consequences of your own actions, they are still not a punishment from an angry, vindictive God. That is not who He is.

If you look at your circumstances and feel condemned, your perspective is not lining up with the Word.

"There is therefore now no condemnation for those who are in

Christ Jesus" (Rom. 8:1).

If you look at your circumstances and are overwhelmed by fear, check your perspective against the Word.

"God gave us a spirit not of fear but of power and love and self-control" (2 Tim. 1:7).

"The LORD is my light and my salvation; whom shall I fear? The LORD is the stronghold of my life; of whom shall I be afraid?" (Ps. 27:1).

"Be strong and courageous. Do not be frightened, and do not be dismayed, for the Lord your God is with you wherever you go" (Josh. 1:9).

If your perspective is making you think that going back to your old life before Christ, to the old you, to the old habits and hang-ups, remember these truths.

"Therefore, if anyone is in Christ, he is a new creation. The old has passed away; behold, the new has come" (2 Cor. 5:17).

"I have been crucified with Christ. It is no longer I who live, but Christ who lives in me. And the life I now live in the flesh I live by faith in the Son of God, who loved me and gave himself for me" (Gal. 2:20).

"Remember not the former things, nor consider the things of old. Behold, I am doing a new thing; now it springs forth, do you not perceive it? I will make a way in the wilderness and rivers in the desert" (Is. 43:18-19).

"I will sprinkle clean water on you, and you shall be clean.... And I will give you a new heart, and a new spirit I will put within you. And I will remove the heart of stone from your flesh and give you a heart of flesh. And I will put my Spirit within you, and cause you to walk in my statutes" (Ez. 36:25-27).

Whatever it is that is coloring your perspective of your circumstances needs to line up with the Word. Worry, fear, condemnation, hopelessness, ungratefulness, disbelief—none of these things line up with the Word. But faith, hope, love, grace, mercy, thankfulness, kindness, self-control, joy, peace—they are a different story.

The Power of Speaking the Word

The Word of God is living and breathing, and it has power. It's God's way of putting things into action. When you speak God's Word, it brings heaven down to earth. It can spur angels into action on your behalf. And it can also help change your perspective and your thinking.

The Bible says that God spoke the world and everything in it into existence.

"And God said, 'Let there be light,' and there was light" (Gen. 1:3).

It is probably a given that God's words are powerful, but the truth is that the words you speak are powerful, too.

"Death and life are in the power of the tongue" (Prov. 18:21).

Your words carry the power of life and death. I want to speak words of life, not words of death. I want my words to build up, not break down. I want my words to give hope, not discouragement. I want to use the power of my words wisely and for the glory of God.

There is power in the spoken word, especially the spoken Word, that is, the Word of God. Whenever you are worried about something or your mind is spinning in circles, trying to figure out how to deal with something, you need to find a scripture that speaks to your situation. I have discovered that when I find a scripture that fits my situation, it allows me to take my out of control thoughts captive and focus them in the right direction.

"We destroy arguments and every lofty opinion raised against the knowledge of God, and take every thought captive to obey Christ" (2 Cor. 10:5).

Speaking that scripture out loud helps because not only am I thinking the scripture, but I am also speaking it and hearing it. It involves more of my senses. It helps the scripture to take root in my heart and my mind. It helps me change my perspective from worry to hope, from fear to courage, from sadness to joy, from the problem to the One who can solve the problem.

"For the word of God is living and active, sharper than any two-edged sword, piercing to the division of soul and of spirit, of joints and of marrow, and discerning the thoughts and intentions of the heart" (Heb. 4:12).

The words you read on the pages of your Bible are not just empty words or words that sound nice. The Word of God is alive. It is active. It does things. It changes things. And when you are struggling with your perspective, it can help you get your thoughts back on the right track. The Greek word for discerning in Hebrews 4:12 is kritikos. It means "skilled in judging…tracing out and passing judgment on the thoughts of the mind."[3] When your mind is racing, when your perspective is skewed, when your attitude is bad, and when you are buying into the lies of the enemy, allow the Word of God to judge the thoughts in your mind. The Word of God itself will help you determine if your perspective lines up with the Word.

And here is another powerful truth, "For as the rain and the snow come down from heaven and do not return there but water the earth, making it bring forth and sprout, giving seed to the sower and bread to the eater, so shall my word be that goes out from my mouth; it shall not return to me empty, but it shall accomplish that which I purpose, and shall succeed in the thing for which I sent it" (Is. 55:10-11.)

God's Word always accomplishes the things God intends for

it to accomplish. Mark 4:20 says, "Those that were sown on the good soil are the ones who hear the word and accept it and bear fruit, thirtyfold and sixtyfold and a hundredfold." If God wants His Word to make you grow and bear fruit, that is what is going to happen.

Psalm 107:20 says, "He sent out his word and healed them." When God sends out His word to heal you, that is exactly what is going to happen.

Romans 10:17 says, "So faith comes from hearing, and hearing through the word of Christ." If God wants His Word to stir and build up your faith, that is exactly what is going to happen.

Deuteronomy 8:3 says, "Man does not live by bread alone, but man lives by every word that comes from the mouth of the LORD." If God wants His Word to feed and nourish your body, soul, and spirit, that is exactly what is going to happen.

His Word gives you victory in the face of temptation.

It sanctifies you and helps keep you pure. "I have stored up your word in my heart, that I might not sin against you" (Ps. 119:11).

"Sanctify them in the truth; your word is truth" (John 17:17).

"How can a young man keep his way pure? By guarding it according to your word" (Ps. 119:9).

The Word guides you and shows you the way to go. "Your word is a lamp to my feet and a light to my path" (Ps. 119:105).

It teaches you, corrects you, equips you, and makes you whole. "All Scripture is breathed out by God and profitable for teaching, for reproof, for correction, and for training in righteousness, that the man of God may be complete, equipped for every good work" (2 Tim. 3:16-17).

The Word of God is incredibly powerful. Don't ever lose sight of that. Filtering the circumstances of your life through the lens of the Word will help you keep your perspective right. When the enemy is attacking you, wield the sword of the Spirit (Eph. 6:17); use the Word of God as your weapon to defeat him. Speak the words of truth that God has implanted in your mind and heart, and thank God, "who gives us the victory through our Lord Jesus Christ" (1 Cor. 15:57).

Promises of God

One of the best parts of the Word of God is all the promises it contains. A promise is "a statement telling someone that you will definitely do something or that something will definitely happen in the future."[4] The Greek word for promise in the Bible carries the sense of blessing, a "divine assurance of good."[5]

When God promises something, it means you can count on it.

> *Filtering the circumstances of your life through the lens of the Word will help you keep your perspective right.*

He is the real deal. He is going to keep His Word. He speaks the truth, and He is the truth. His Word comes with a guarantee.

"For all the promises of God in Him are Yes, and in Him Amen, to the glory of God through us" (2 Cor. 1:20, NKJV).

"He who promised is faithful" (Heb. 10:23"

"His divine power has granted to us all things that pertain to life and godliness, through the knowledge of him who called us to his own glory and excellence, by which he has granted to us his precious and very great promises" (2 Pet. 1:3-5).

You can count on God. Because of Jesus, the promises of God are yours. When I am struggling to keep things in perspective, I remind myself of the powerful promises in the Word. One of my favorites is Isaiah 40:30-31. "Even youths shall faint and be weary, and young men shall fall exhausted; but they who wait for the LORD shall renew their strength; they shall mount up with wings like eagles; they shall run and not be weary; they shall walk and not faint."

Another favorite is Psalm 91:1-16.

He who dwells in the shelter of the Most High will abide in the shadow of the Almighty. I will say to the LORD, "My refuge and my fortress, my God, in whom I trust.

For he will deliver you from the snare of the fowler and from the deadly pestilence. He will cover you with his pinions, and under his wings you will find refuge; his faithfulness is a shield and buckler. You will not fear the terror of the night, nor the arrow that flies by day, nor the pestilence that stalks in darkness, nor the destruction that wastes at noonday.

A thousand may fall at your side, ten thousand at your right hand, but it will not come near you. You will only look with your eyes and see the recompense of the wicked.

Because you have made the LORD your dwelling place—the Most High, who is my refuge—no evil shall be allowed to befall you, no plague come near your tent.

For he will command his angels concerning you to guard you in all your ways. On their hands they will bear you up, lest you strike your foot against a stone. You will tread on the lion and the adder; the young lion and the serpent you will trample underfoot.

"Because he holds fast to me in love, I will deliver him;
I will protect him, because he knows my name. When
he calls to me, I will answer him; I will be with him in
trouble; I will rescue him and honor him. With long life
I will satisfy him and show him my salvation.

Reminding myself of God's promises, reading them, speaking
them out loud, and sharing them with others helps me to keep
my eyes on Jesus instead of my circumstances. His promises give
me victory over the attempts of the enemy to defeat me. Are there
times I am frustrated with the delay in the fulfillment of God's
promises to me? Of course. But God's timing is just that— God's
timing. Just because it is not my timing does not mean the promise
is not true. I have peace in my heart that His Word is 100 percent
true, and I will continue to hold fast to His promises to me.

Something that can be really helpful is to keep a promise list
in a notebook or a journal. When you are reading the Bible, and a
promise jumps out at you or really speaks to your heart, take the
time to add it to your promise list. When you are struggling or feeling discouraged, you can get out your promise list and read it over,
quickly getting a hefty dose of truth and encouragement.

For example, if you struggle with fear, your promise list might
include some of these verses.

"In peace I will both lie down and sleep; for you alone, O
LORD, make me dwell in safety" (Ps. 4:8).

"God gave us a spirit not of fear but of power and love and
self-control" (2 Tim. 1:7).

"So we can confidently say, 'The Lord is my helper; I will not
fear; what can man do to me?'" (Heb. 13:6).

"Behold, God is my salvation; I will trust, and will not be afraid; for the LORD GOD is my strength and my song, and he has become my salvation" (Is. 12:2).

Your promise list doesn't have to be about a specific issue. Just write down any promises that the Lord quickens to your spirit when you are reading or that resonate in your heart and mind. Your promise list will become a valuable resource for you in times of trouble or doubt. Please see the appendix for a list of my favorite promises from the Word of God.

Your perspective matters. Making a conscious effort to keep a positive perspective that lines up with the Word of God will make a big difference in your life, especially when you are facing challenging circumstances. If you have developed a habit of being negative, it might take some effort to change your perspective, but it is worth it. Keep taking those thoughts captive to the obedience of Christ. Find the promises of God that speak to your situation and stand on them, speak them aloud, and even remind God of what He promised. You have hope because He who promised is faithful. Never forget that.

"You keep him in perfect peace whose mind is stayed on you, because he trusts in you. Trust in the LORD forever, for the LORD GOD is an everlasting rock" (Is. 26:3-4).

On the Other Hand

CHAPTER TEN

Moving Forward

When I came to realize that life here on earth is really just a blip but, life in heaven is forever, it helped change my perspective about what really mattered. Life on earth is just temporary. The Bible compares our lives to grass that withers away or flowers that fade. "All flesh is grass, and all its beauty is like the flower of the field. The grass withers, the flower fades when the breath of the LORD blows on it; surely the people are grass. The grass withers, the flower fades, but the word of our God will stand forever" (Is. 40:6-8).

Keeping my perspective right helps me appreciate the small things in life. I don't need to focus on the waiting. I need to trust God to handle all the details, especially the big things, such as my healing. I don't need to worry or be afraid because He has it all under control.

> Therefore I tell you, do not be anxious about your life, what you will eat or what you will drink, nor about your body, what you will put on....Look at the birds of the air: they neither sow nor reap nor gather into barns, and yet your heavenly Father feeds them. Are you not of more value than they? And which of you by

being anxious can add a single hour to his span of life? And why are you anxious about clothing? Consider the lilies of the field, how they grow: they neither toil nor spin, yet I tell you, even Solomon in all his glory was not arrayed like one of these....But seek first the kingdom of God and his righteousness, and all these things will be added to you. Therefore do not be anxious about tomorrow, for tomorrow will be anxious for itself. Sufficient for the day is its own trouble. (Matt. 6:25-29, 33-34)

"Don't worry about anything; instead, pray about everything; tell God your needs, and don't forget to thank him for his answers" (Phil. 4:6, TLB).

There have been many times I needed to ask forgiveness for worrying instead of trusting. God forgave me and gave me a clean slate so I could move forward, trusting Him for everything. Just like the Scripture says, if He takes care of the birds and the flowers, how much more will He take care of me? I am made in the image of God (Gen. 1:26-27). I am His daughter (1 John 3:1).

I have been adopted into His family (Eph. 1:5). I am the apple of His eye (Zech. 2:8). Not one hair of my head falls out without God knowing about it (Luke 12:7). He knows every detail of my body, every detail of my mind, and every detail of my spirit. I am His, and He is mine (Song of Sol. 2:16). He loves me without condition and without question, so I can trust Him without condition and without question.

The most important thing in life is your relationship with God. The truth is that you can never really move forward in having a purpose-filled and purpose-driven life until you are in right relationship with the Lord who created you and loves you and gave Himself as a sacrifice for your redemption. We have all sinned and fallen short of the glory of God (Rom. 3:23). And sin separates us from God if we have not accepted Jesus Christ as our Savior and received the forgiveness, grace, and mercy He died to give us. My hope and prayer is that you have accepted God's free gift of salvation and surrendered your life to Christ. But if not, I encourage you to go back and read the section "How You Can Have Hope" in chapter 6. No matter your circumstances, you need God in your life to truly move forward.

Out with the Old, In with the New

My life has not been easy. I am sure many of you can say the same thing. Becoming a quadriplegic as a teenager completely changed the trajectory of my life. But in the face of tragedy, in the face of challenging circumstances, in the face of trials and troubles, we all have a choice. We can choose to stay stuck, wound up in the drama of whatever it is we are facing, or we can choose to move forward, to passionately pursue God's plan for our lives, trusting that whatever it is we are facing is part of His plan. I chose to move forward. You can, too.

Now, there are obviously physical issues and circumstances that are beyond our natural ability to leave behind or

> *You have been accepted, redeemed, and forgiven. Don't let anyone tell you otherwise.*

address. But the truth is that it is not usually something physical that keeps us from moving forward. It is usually all the emotional and spiritual baggage we carry around like so much junk that holds us back, keeps us stagnant, and prevents us from moving forward.

But when you give your life to Christ, when you are born again, you become a new creation.

"Therefore, if anyone is in Christ, he is a new creation; old things have passed away; behold, all things have become new" (2 Cor. 5:17, NKJV).

And when you become a new creation, Jesus makes all things new. Don't miss the power of that phrase: all things. Jesus doesn't make just a few things or even most things new. He makes all things new. That means you don't have to carry around all that emotional and spiritual baggage from your past. You can let go of the guilt, shame, fear, condemnation, bitterness, hatred, envy, strife, jealousy, rebellion, anger, and all the other things that keep you bound to your past and prevent you from moving forward. God makes all things new. You have been accepted, redeemed, and forgiven. Don't let anyone tell you otherwise.

But you have a part to play. God has set you free, but you have to choose to walk in that freedom. It's like the woman sitting in prison when she is really free which we talked about in Chapter 1.

"Awake, awake! Put on your strength....Shake yourself from the dust, arise....Loose yourself from the bonds of your neck, O captive daughter of Zion!" (Is. 52:1–2, NKJV).

You may be used to your bondage, to the chains that have bound you for so long. But God has set you free. The Lord has

> *God has set you free, but you have to choose to walk in that freedom.*

unlocked your shackles and opened the prison door. You are free, but you must decide to loose those chains of the past, shake off the dirt and dust, and take hold of that freedom.

God has made you new, but you need to choose to put on that new self. And you can't put on the new until you take off the old.

"You have heard about him and were taught in him, as the truth is in Jesus, to put off your old self, which belongs to your former manner of life and is corrupt through deceitful desires, and to be renewed in the spirit of your minds, and to put on the new self, created after the likeness of God in true righteousness and holiness" (Eph. 4:21-24).

Renewing your mind is a big part of putting off the old and putting on the new. Our thoughts are what tend to keep us tied to the past. That is why it is so important to read and meditate on the Word of God. Second Corinthians 10:5 talks about taking every thought captive to the obedience of Christ. I have mentioned that verse several times because taking your thoughts captive to the obedience of Christ is a key habit—for your attitude, for your perspective, for walking in freedom, for gaining victory over the enemy, and so many other things. But you can't take your thoughts captive and make sure they are lining up with the truth of what Jesus says if you don't actually know what Jesus says. When you take hold of your thoughts and make sure they line up with the Word of God, it renews your mind. It trains your brain to think differently. It helps you keep things in the right perspective. And this renewal of your mind comes with another important benefit: it transforms you.

"Do not be conformed to this world, but be transformed by the renewal of your mind, that by testing you may discern what is the will of God, what is good and acceptable and perfect" (Rom. 12:2).

The Greek word for transformed in Romans 12:2 is metamorphoō.[1] The word is where we get words like metamorphose and metamorphosis. It refers to undergoing a complete change. That is the power of the Word of God. It can completely change you, especially your thinking. So, if you are struggling with putting off the old and putting on the new, start by renewing your mind. Start by digging into the Bible and letting God's living, powerful Word change the way you think.

When you become a believer in Christ Jesus as your Savior, you are forgiven and redeemed from all the stuff in your past. You are a new creation. All things have become new. The old stuff is gone. So leave all the stuff connected with your old self in the past and move forward. Renew your mind with the Word of God, and put on your new self, the one that is like Jesus.

It is for freedom that God set you free (Gal. 5:1). You can't let your past or any circumstance of your life keep you in bondage. Follow hard after God and His purposes for your life. Allow Him to guide your steps as you pursue His purposes for your life, and walk in the freedom He died to give you.

How I Found Hope for My Future

To move forward, you need to have hope. You need to focus on Jesus, the author and finisher of your faith. Life is like a race that everyone is running. You won't run well, and you will never get to the finish line if you keep looking behind you. So, instead look to Jesus.

"Therefore we also, since we are surrounded by so great a cloud of witnesses, let us lay aside every weight, and the sin which so easily ensnares us, and let us run with endurance the race that is set before us, looking unto Jesus, the author and finisher of our faith" (Heb. 12:1-2, NKJV).

Jesus is my living hope. I fix my eyes on Him, knowing that He is in control of my life and that He has a wonderful plan for me. I focus on what can be instead of focusing on my circumstances. I look ahead, not behind. Even though I am paralyzed, I can still be excited about life. My paralysis doesn't define me. I am determined to enjoy this life God has given me in every way I can. Just because I am paralyzed does not mean that I have to sit at home feeling sorry for myself every day. I have a full life. I do things that I enjoy. For my last birthday, I went out to dinner with my two best friends from high school. We went to Cielo Blue Mexican Grill and Cantina. I had tacos, and some cheese dip, and they were amazing. Who doesn't love cheese dip? I have an amazing family and amazing friends, and I am not going to let any of the opportunities God has given me pass me by. I know that God has a plan for me. I know I have a future here on earth and an even better future in heaven. How could I not have hope?

Several years ago, I went to Colorado Springs with my mom and my caregiver. It was a wonderful trip. We made several stops along the way, including Memphis, Tennessee, where we saw several of Elvis Presley's homes. But the best part was Colorado Springs. The mountains are absolutely breathtaking. We could see the Rocky Mountains from where we were staying. They were beautiful. God created some amazing things. It is no wonder that the angels in the throne room of heaven cry out, "Holy, holy, holy is the LORD of hosts; the whole earth is full of his glory!" (Isa. 6:3). When I look out at the breathtaking majesty of this world the Lord created, I can't help but agree; the whole earth is indeed full of His glory.

Personally, when I am out in the world to enjoy the magnificent sights of God's creation, I prefer being in the valley to being on the mountaintop. I like to look up in wonder at the majesty of the mountains before me. And that is a good perspective for life. When you are in the valley, look up. Look to God, the Maker of heaven and earth. Lift your eyes up to the mountains and be reminded of who your Helper is.

I will lift up my eyes to the hills—from whence comes my help? My help comes from the LORD, who made heaven and earth. He will not allow your foot to be moved; He who keeps you will not slumber. Behold, He who keeps Israel shall neither slumber nor sleep. The LORD is your keeper; the LORD is your shade at your right hand. The sun shall not strike you by day, nor the moon by night. The LORD shall preserve you from all evil; He shall preserve your soul. The LORD shall preserve your going out and your coming in from this time forth, and even forevermore. (Ps. 121, NKJV)

> *When you are in the valley, look up. Look to God, the Maker of heaven and earth. Lift your eyes up to the mountains and be reminded of who your Helper is.*

Taking time to enjoy creation is one of the things that reminds me of how much God loves me and how He orchestrates every detail perfectly. I especially love waterfalls. The beauty, the way they sound—whether it is a gentle trickle or resounding roar—they take my breath away. They are my favorite thing in all of creation.

"Deep calls to deep at the roar of your waterfalls; all your breakers and your waves have gone over me. By day the LORD commands his steadfast love, and at night his song is with me, a prayer to the God of my life" (Ps. 42:7-8).

Waterfalls are just one more reminder of God's amazing love for me. Even though sending His Son to die on a cross for my sins was the greatest act of love ever and would have been enough for me to know how much God loves me, He has never ceased to show me how much He loves me. In big things and small things, God has showered me with His love, and I can have hope, the confident expectation kind, because I am secure in my heavenly Father's love.

The fact that God has shown Himself strong on my behalf as my provider has been another source of hope for me. When the funds for my care were in question, God worked it all out, just as He has provided for all my other needs. In Genesis 22:14, the Lord is called Jehovah Jireh, meaning the Lord will provide. A provider is who God is; it is part of His character. And what is so interesting about this revelation of God's character is that occurred on the heels of something that didn't make sense in the natural. And that gives me hope as well.

You see, in Genesis 22, God had asked Abraham to sacrifice his son—the son God had promised him, the miracle boy Abraham and his wife Sarah had waited on for years and years, the son who

> *Even in the midst of something that made no sense in the natural, the supernatural was at work.*

was the fulfillment of God's covenant with Abraham. It made no sense for God to ask Abraham to sacrifice him. But God's ways are not ours, and we don't think like He does because we can't see the timeline of all eternity the way He does.

"For as the heavens are higher than the earth, so are my ways higher than your ways and my thoughts than your thoughts" (Is. 55:9).

But even in the midst of something that made no sense in the natural, the supernatural was at work. It was all part of God's eternal plan, not only for Abraham and Isaac but for you and me as well. God provided a lamb to take Isaac's place, just as He provided the Lamb (Jesus) to take my place and your place and the place of every other person who accepts the saving work of Jesus on the cross. So even when things don't make sense to my finite human brain, I can trust that God is still working things out according to His plan. He will still provide. He will still love me with the perfect love of a perfect Father. He is and will always be my living hope.

And because of that hope, I can believe for better days. I can trust God on the timing of the days when I will once again walk and run and dance. And no matter how challenging my circumstances, I will keep trusting and serving the Lord because the truth is that one day with Him is better than a thousand days without Him.

> How lovely is your dwelling place, O LORD of hosts!
> My soul longs, yes, faints for the courts of the LORD;
> my heart and flesh sing for joy to the living God....
> Blessed are those whose strength is in you....As they
> go through the Valley...they make it a place of springs;
> the early rain also covers it with pools. They go from
> strength to strength....For a day in your courts is better
> than a thousand elsewhere. I would rather be a door-
> keeper in the house of my God than dwell in the tents
> of wickedness. For the LORD God is a sun and shield;
> the LORD bestows favor and honor. No good thing
> does he withhold from those who walk uprightly. O
> LORD of hosts, blessed is the one who trusts in you!
> (Ps. 84:1-2, 5-7, 10-12)

Learning to Trust God Through Each Day

When I was learning how to live my best life as a quadriplegic, I didn't dread each day; I enjoyed it. While there were many challenges to face, I was able to trust God to help me meet them head-on. And even though being a quadriplegic presents many difficulties, I am thankful that I live in the time that I do. Not only was I able to survive my injury, but I have also been able to thrive and be much more independent because of the technology available to me. Being able to use a computer was huge for me because of the ability to communicate with others, read, learn, play games, and so many other things that would have been impossible for a quad not too many years ago. Being injured in this day and age was a blessing because I still have so many things I can do because of technology.

My trust in God has also grown so much through seeing small answers to prayer. The answer to little everyday prayers helped me learn to trust God for all things. For example, there have been times when I couldn't find something important, but after I prayed about it, all of a sudden, the thing I needed to find would be right there. I was exercising my faith muscle by praying and trusting God for the small things in life. I think sometimes we make the mistake of thinking God doesn't want us to bother Him with small or simple things. When we have a headache, we suffer through it or take a pain reliever rather than asking God to heal it. When we lose our keys, we spend half an hour retracing our steps, dumping out our purses, and checking under all the couch cushions, and it doesn't occur to us to ask God for help until our own efforts have failed. But God is a good Father. He doesn't care just about the big stuff. He cares about the little stuff, too, and He wants His kids to come to Him when they are hurting or need help, no matter how big or small the need, the way any good father would.

As I said before, when you start by trusting God for the small things, it is a whole lot easier to trust Him for the big things. It is much easier to trust God to heal your cancer when you have experienced His healing your headache when you asked. When you have prayed and asked God to provide the funds to pay your phone bill, and He came through, it is much easier to trust Him for the five thousand dollars for a new transmission in your car.

As things such as finding something I lost when I prayed about it continued to happen, my faith grew and developed. It also made me a woman of prayer. I don't want to trust God for just certain things. I want to trust Him for the big things and the small things. I want to run to Him when I am hurting or need help, trusting that my Father is waiting and wanting me to come to Him. I want to seek His direction for my life on a regular basis. I want to know His will for me and see it come to pass in my life.

Trusting God every day is one of the ways I exercise my faith muscle. I rely on God to get me through every day. Proverbs 3:5-6 says, "Trust in the LORD with all your heart, and do not lean on your own understanding. In all your ways acknowledge him, and he will make straight your paths." Not leaning on your own understanding is a big part of trusting God. If I have my plan and my way of doing things, and I expect God to adjust His plans accordingly, I am not trusting Him. Even when things don't seem to make sense, you still need to trust God and allow Him to direct your paths so you can move forward. He can see way farther ahead than you can, so trust Him instead of trying to control and direct everything yourself. When you try to control things yourself, you may end up veering off the path or even going backward when you think you are really going straight ahead. Keep your focus on Jesus. Trust Him, and you will keep moving forward in God's plans and purposes for your life.

When you trust God, it makes you strong. It helps keep you

right smack in the middle of His will for your life. It helps you keep your perspective right because it keeps Jesus at the center of your thoughts.

"The LORD is my strength and my shield; in him my heart trusts, and I am helped; my heart exults, and with my song I give thanks to him" (Ps. 28:7).

"Those who trust in the LORD are like Mount Zion, which cannot be moved, but abides forever" (Ps. 125:1).

And as if that weren't enough, when you trust God, your heart and mind can be at peace, knowing that He has everything under control.

"You keep him in perfect peace whose mind is stayed on you, because he trusts in you" (Is. 26:3).

When you have inner peace about something, you can trust that it is the right way to go. Trust means you are secure in the Lord and secure in your faith, knowing He will lead you in the right direction. You know that He will guide you wherever you need to go. He will help you move forward.

Encouraging Words

If you are struggling to move forward, to leave the past behind, to put off the old and put on the new, a little encouragement may be just what you need. We all need encouragement as we face both the day-to-day struggles of ordinary life as well as the seemingly insurmountable obstacles we face at times. And the best place to get encouragement is from the Lord.

First Samuel 30:6 (MEV) says, "David was greatly distressed, for the people talked of stoning him.... But David encouraged himself in the LORD his God." David was obviously facing a difficult situation—people wanted him dead! But David knew exactly what to do. He knew exactly where to turn. He turned to the Lord and found the encouragement he needed to get through the trial he was facing.

> *Fastening your heart and mind upon the Lord gives you the strength and encouragement you need in times of distress.*

The Hebrew word translated as "encouraged" in 1 Samuel 30:6 is hāzaq. It means to strengthen, to prevail, to be resolute, to be secure, to make bold, to be courageous, and to withstand.[2] When you are facing challenges, that is the kind of encouragement you need— encouragement that makes you strong, secure, courageous, bold, and resolute; encouragement that fills you with the knowledge and trust that you will prevail and withstand whatever it is you are facing. But hāzaq also means to fasten upon.[3] It reminds me of the meaning of the Hebrew word for wait: to be bound together with.

"They who wait for the LORD shall renew their strength; they shall mount up with wings like eagles; they shall run and not be weary; they shall walk and not faint" (Is. 40:31).

Just like being bound together with the Lord gives you the strength you need during your waiting season, fastening your heart and mind upon the Lord gives you the strength and encouragement you need in times of distress. The more closely connected you are to the Lord, the easier it is to navigate the seasons of life, whether they are seasons of waiting, trials, growth, or any other season you may experience.

So, how do you encourage yourself in the Lord? You spend time with Him in prayer and in worship. You also spend time in His Word, searching the Scripture for the words of life, the words of

> ## *Your hope has a target.*

hope, the words of promise, and the words of strength you need for the particular situation or season you are facing. Scripture is full of hope and strength. Your hope has a target; you are not just hoping in nothing.

"Why are you cast down, O my soul, and why are you in turmoil within me? Hope in God; for I shall again praise him, my salvation and my God" (Ps. 42:11).

"You are my hiding place and my shield; I hope in your word" (Ps. 119:114).

"May the God of hope fill you with all joy and peace in believing, so that by the power of the Holy Spirit you may abound in hope" (Rom. 15:13).

"The name of the LORD is a strong tower; the righteous man runs into it and is safe" (Prov. 18:10).

"Be strong and courageous. Do not be frightened, and do not be dismayed, for the LORD your God is with you wherever you go" (Josh. 1:9).

"In all these things we are more than conquerors through him who loved us" (Rom. 8:37).

Don't give up hope. Keep moving forward. Try and try again on things; just because something didn't work out the first time doesn't mean it won't happen. Keep putting off the old and putting on the new. Remember that God has made you a new creation and has made all things new. And when God does close a door, know that it is because He has something better for you. Keep trusting God, even when things don't seem to make sense. Always remember to take it one day at a time as you move forward, and keep your focus in the right place. Don't focus on the what-ifs and the what might be. Focus on God. And don't forget to pray. Be a man or woman of prayer. It makes a difference.

CHAPTER ELEVEN

Dance!

I love almost anything that has to do with dance. I took dance classes, from ballet to jazz, from the age of four until I was fourteen. I stopped dance classes when I got more involved with cheerleading, but even within that dance was still involved. As a cheerleader, I did many different dance routines. Dancing was a way I could just soak in the music and release all my emotions--positive, negative, and everything in between--while disappearing into my own little world. Dancing gave me a sense of freedom. I loved it.

When you look at me now, you may think that I no longer dance, but you couldn't be more wrong. While I may not be able to tap my feet or move my arms, I am still dancing on the inside. And I am going to keep dancing through life.

Reason to Dance

People dance for many reasons. They dance to celebrate. They dance to express themselves. They dance to compete or to perform. They dance to exercise. They dance to have fun. They dance to worship the Lord.

One of my favorite quotes is, "Life isn't about waiting for the storm to pass. It's about learning how to dance in the rain."[1] I love the quote because it captures the essence of rejoicing despite your circumstances. I have always been a positive person. When bad circumstances come my way, I may be down for a minute, but I have always been able to bounce back quickly. That has been a blessing in my life because being paralyzed isn't something you can just make go away or deal with using a quick fix. If I had chosen to wait for the storm of my paralysis to pass, I would still be waiting, and I would have wasted the precious life God has given me.

You have to ride out the storm no matter how long it lasts. But there is more to facing storms than just learning to endure them. You need to find joy in the midst of every circumstance, "for the joy of the LORD is your strength" (Neh. 8:10). Your circumstances do not have to control your emotions. The storm may be raging, and the rain may be pouring down, but you can learn how to stay positive and focus on what is good in your life. I choose to focus on the positive. I choose to focus on all the wonderful things about this precious gift of life God has given me. Why should I live a miserable life, feeling depressed, sad, and hurting all the time, when instead I can choose to dance through it and make the absolute best of it?

I encourage you to do the same. When you look to Jesus as your source of hope, your source of joy, your source of peace, and your source of strength, you will discover you have the ability to dance in the rain, too. So, no matter what is going on in your life, turn on some music and dance your heart out. Release all your inhibitions. Just let go and dance like no one is watching. It will release stress and worry as you wiggle, jiggle, jump, and jive your way into happiness and joy!

And don't be afraid to dance as an act of worship. Worship is powerful when you are in the midst of a storm because it shifts your focus off of yourself and onto the Lord who loves you, has a plan for you, gives you strength, shelters you, protects you, guides you, fills your heart with the peace that passes all understanding, and promises that with Him nothing will impossible. So dance! Worship the Lord by dancing. "Praise his name with dancing" (Ps. 149:3). Be like King David, who "danced before the LORD with all his might...leaping and dancing before the LORD" (2 Sam. 6:14, 16). When David's wife Michal saw David dancing and criticized him for it, his response was, "I will be even more undignified than this" (2 Sam. 6:22, NKJV). Although he was a king, David recognized who the King of kings was, and it was not him. David knew that God was worthy of all his praise, so he praised the Lord "with all his might." When David recognized the goodness of God, his feet just wouldn't stay still.

When the goodness of God moves you, don't stifle it. If the goodness of God moves your heart so that it overflows out of your eyes, let those tears fall. If it moves your mouth to sing praises to His name, even if you can't carry a tune in a bucket, you can still make a joyful noise (Ps. 100:1). And when the goodness of God moves your feet to dance before Him with all your might, let loose. It is OK to be undignified. God loves your worship, even if you have no rhythm. So dance!

Let Jesus Lead

There is another aspect to dancing in the Bible that you may not be aware of. First Peter 4:10-11 says this, "As each has received a gift, use it to serve one another, as good stewards of God's varied grace...whoever serves, as one who serves by the strength that God supplies—in order that in everything God may be glorified through Jesus Christ. To him belong glory and dominion forever and ever. Amen."

I know you are probably wondering what in the world that verse has to do with dancing. The truth is that it is one of the most powerful verses in the whole Bible about dancing. The Greek word translated as "supplies" is chorēgeō. It has the same root word as the English word choreography. It means to be a dance leader.[2]

> *When you allow God to lead in how you use those gifts, the result will be the most amazing, awe-inspiring, breathtaking use of your gifts.*

God has specific gifts and abilities specially designed just for you, as well as the plans and purposes He has for you on earth. Because of those gifts and abilities, you have been equipped to do amazing things. And because God gives good gifts to His children, you can choose to use those gifts in your strength and follow your own purposes, and you will likely be able to accomplish many wonderful things. But that is not the best way to use your gifts.

Think of it this way: let's say you are a wonderful dancer. God has given you an incredible natural talent as a dancer, and you have practiced, studied, and rehearsed for years and years to develop and hone your skills. You are especially good at the tango. When you dance, it is amazing. But then let's say you are given the opportunity to dance with the man who is the best dancer of the tango the world has ever seen—not only that, he actually invented the tango. There has never been and never will be anyone better at it than he is. If you are given the opportunity to dance with him and you let him lead, it will be the most amazing, awe-inspiring, breathtaking version of the tango you will ever dance.

It's like that with the gifts and abilities God has given you. You can practice, study, and rehearse for years and years to develop and hone your skills, and when you use them, it can be amazing. But when you allow God—the One who created you, gave you those gifts and abilities, and in fact invented them and knows how to use them better than anyone in the world—to lead in how you use those gifts, the result will be the most amazing, awe-inspiring, breathtaking use of your gifts.

That is one of the ways that I can still dance. Physically, I can still move my head and shoulders in time to the music. When I hear music, I can still close my eyes and picture myself rocking out to my favorite 80s songs. I can still express the joy in my heart through the physical abilities I still have and the imaginings of my mind and heart. But beyond all that, I can choose to follow the lead of my Lord and Savior in the dance of using the gifts and abilities He has given me. By allowing Him to lead the dance, I can glorify Him and take the utmost joy in using the gifts He has given me.

And even if you have two left feet, you can dance the same way. God has given you special gifts and talents. Let Jesus lead you in your dance. Take His hand, and dance your heart out with Him, honoring Him in the way you use your gifts by allowing Him to lead.

Choose Joy

Dance is often an expression of joy. Sometimes, when joy fills your heart, you can't help but move your feet (or head and shoulders in my case these days). Joy is one of those things that are often misunderstood. Joy and happiness are not the same. Happiness is directly connected to your circumstances, whereas joy is independent of them. In the midst of a crisis or a storm, it is obviously difficult to be happy, but you can have joy during the crises and storms of life. Joy is something cultivated deep inside your soul as you walk with Jesus. When you choose to rejoice in the Lord, no matter the trial or hardship, seeds of joy take root in your heart. When you look to the joy of the Lord to be your strength when you are facing difficulties, those seeds begin to grow, and the roots go down deep into your soul. And every time you choose joy, your heart gets stronger, your faith gets stronger, and you get stronger.

As if that weren't enough, joy has another very important quality: it is everlasting.

"And the ransomed of the LORD shall return and come to Zion with singing; everlasting joy shall be upon their heads; they shall obtain gladness and joy, and sorrow and sighing shall flee away" (Is. 51:11, Emphasis Added).

> "The Spirit of the LORD God is upon Me, because the LORD has anointed Me to preach good tidings to the poor; He has sent Me to heal the brokenhearted, to proclaim liberty to the captives, and the opening of the prison to those who are bound…to comfort all who mourn…to give them beauty for ashes, the oil of joy for mourning, the garment of praise for the spirit of heaviness; that they may be called trees of righteousness, the planting of the Lord, that He may be glorified."…But you shall be named the priests of the LORD, they shall call you the servants of our God.…Instead of your shame you shall have double honor, and instead of confusion they shall rejoice in their portion. Therefore in their land they shall possess double; everlasting joy shall be theirs. (Is. 61:1-3, 6-7, NKJV, Emphasis Added).

The second passage from Isaiah is the one Jesus read a portion of in the synagogue and declared that it was fulfilled in the hearing of the people gathered there (Luke 4:21). That means Jesus came not only to heal the brokenhearted and set the captives free but also to give them— and give to you and me—everlasting joy. What an amazing promise!

Joy is also a fruit of the Spirit. That means if you have the Holy Spirit living inside you, the fruit in your life includes joy—guaranteed. It's one of the things I love about the fruit of the Spirit. The verses say this, "But the fruit of the Spirit is love, joy, peace, patience, kindness, goodness, faithfulness, gentleness, self-control; against such things there is no law" (Gal. 5:22-23).

Notice that it uses the word fruit, not fruits. If they were fruits, it would imply that God might pick and choose which ones you get. You might get patience and kindness, while I get goodness and gentleness. But that is not how it works. It is fruit. It is a package deal. That means you get it all: love, peace, patience, kindness, goodness, faithfulness, gentleness, self-control, and, of course, joy.

You can have joy no matter your circumstances. No matter the storm, no matter the trial, when you have the Holy Spirit within you, you have joy. Choose to walk in it. You can dance in the rain.

Choose Happiness

While we are on the subject of choosing, you can also choose to be happy. While there are obvious times when you won't be happy, such as when you lose a loved one, or you are in the fieriest part of a trial, you don't have to be unhappy any time you face a challenge or weather a storm. You do not have to let your circumstances define you or control your emotions.

While I was obviously not happy that I ended up paralyzed after my accident, I made a choice that I was not going to let my

> *Shake off the chains of your past, shake off the chains of defeat and discouragement, shake off the chains of sadness and sorrow, and get up and dance!*

condition control my life. Does my life have challenges? Absolutely. Do I face storms? You bet. Do I get impatient for God to get me out of this chair? You know I do. But I still choose to be content with the life God has given me. I know He has a purpose. I know He has a plan. And I know His timing is perfect. The Word says that "godliness with contentment is great gain" (1 Tim. 6:6). That is where I am.

The Hebrew word for happy in the Bible is 'ešer. It is used in verses such as "Happy is he who has the God of Jacob for his help, whose hope is in the LORD his God" (Ps. 146:5, NKJV). The word means and is often translated as "blessed."[3] I think that concept is the key to choosing happiness. We need to recognize that even in difficult and challenging circumstances, we are still blessed. Each of us has blessings, both big and small, that can help us keep our perspective right and help us not allow our circumstances to control our emotions.

You have a choice. You can choose to stay in bondage to your emotions, living in prison and allowing doubt, fear, sadness, unbelief, and countless other emotions to control you and drive your happiness away. Or you can choose to loose yourself from the bonds of your neck and walk—no, dance in the freedom Jesus set you free for. It is your choice. Choose freedom. Choose life. Choose abundant life. Jesus came to set the captives free, and that includes you. So shake off the chains of your past, shake off the chains of defeat and discouragement, shake off the chains of sadness and sorrow, and get up and dance!

Time to Dance

The Bible says that there is a season and a time for everything.

> For everything there is a season, and a time for every matter under heaven: a time to be born, and a time to die; a time to plant, and a time to pluck up what is planted; a time to kill, and a time to heal; a time to break down, and a time to build up; a time to weep, and a time to laugh; a time to mourn, and a time to dance; a time to cast away stones, and a time to gather stones together; a time to embrace, and a time to refrain from embracing; a time to seek, and a time to lose; a time to keep, and a time to cast away; a time to tear, and a time to sew; a time to keep silence, and a time to speak; a time to love, and a time to hate; a time for war, and a time for peace. (Eccl. 3:1-8)

There is a time to dance. And the time to dance is now! Whether you are dancing in joy, dancing in worship, or dancing as you use your God-given gifts, this is your time. Dance! Don't waste the precious time God has given you. Seize the opportunities God has given you, and live the abundant life you were created for.

Remember that it is hard to dance if you are carrying a bunch of baggage or if you are weighed down by burdens. Bring all that baggage and all those burdens to the foot of the cross and hand them over to Jesus to deal with, and then take His outstretched hand as He asks you to dance with Him. For that is your purpose:

to have a relationship with the Lord God Almighty, who created you, who loves you, and who delights in having you as His child, and to glorify Him forever.

> ## *The time to dance is now!*

Yes, storms and battles and challenges and difficulties will come. We all face them. But when you are bound together with the Lord, when you wait on Him, when you have the Holy Spirit and see His fruit in your life, you will have all the strength you need to face whatever comes. And you can be at peace knowing that God has everything under control, that He is working out His plans and purposes for your life, and that nothing is too hard for Him. That means you can dance through the difficulties. Then, when you win the battle, you can dance yet again as an act of worship to the Lord God, Maker of heaven and earth, the Lord your provider, the Lord your healer, the Lord your peace, the Comforter, the Lamb of God who takes away the sins of the world, the light of the world, your heavenly Father, the Good Shepherd—and the One who leads you in the dance.

About the Author

Jessica Lane brings you her story of hope in the face of life's challenges in her debut book "On The Other Hand."

Just two months after her 16th birthday, Jessica was paralyzed in a car crash. Life for this active teenager was changed in a flash. Her body would no longer turn round-off back handsprings or carry her across the finish line of the 200m race. The severity of her injury left her without mobility below the shoulders.

Jessica demonstrated her tenacious spirit throughout her recovery. She defied all expectations when she was weaned off of the ventilator to breathe on her own again. She returned to school after six months at Shepherd Center and graduated on time with her class at Parkview High School in Lilburn, Ga. After high school, Jessica became a certified interior designer.

While she loved working in design, her heart was really bent on helping people and serving as an encouragement to others. Jessica completed the counseling course Caring for People God's Way and decided to focus on ministry. She launched her blog Renewing Strength (www.jessicalane.org) based on Isaiah 40:30-31 "Even youths grow tired and weary, and young men stumble and fall; but those who hope in the LORD will renew their strength. They will soar on wings like eagles; they will run and not grow weary, they will walk and not be faint."

Jessica has spent the last three decades learning to navigate myriad challenges while striving to honor God in the process. Jessica offers perspectives gained and lessons learned to encourage and inspire you as you follow God's plan for your life.

Jessica lives in Atlanta, GA.

Photo Memories

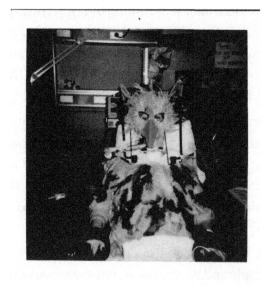

When Jessica's mom dressed her up as a bird for Halloween by using her halo device and string as the cage.

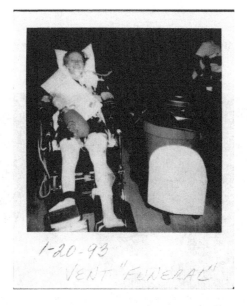

1-20-93
VENT "FUNERAL"

The vent funeral on January 20, 1993, was when Jessica could finally breathe 100 % on her own without it!

During the March '93 snowstorm, I didn't have access to my wheelchair while the power was out so this was my chair.

When Jessica graduated with her class in 1995.

Appendix

Favorite Promises from the Word of God

Saying, "If you will diligently listen to the voice of the LORD your God, and do that which is right in his eyes, and give ear to his commandments and keep all his statutes, I will put none of the diseases on you that I put on the Egyptians, for I am the LORD, your healer."

—EXODUS 15:26

The LORD your God has chosen you…for his treasured possession.

—DEUTERONOMY 7:6

Be strong and courageous. Do not be frightened, and do not be dismayed, for the LORD your God is with you wherever you go.

—JOSHUA 1:9

The joy of the LORD is your strength.

—NEHEMIAH 8:10

Blessed is the man who walks not in the counsel of the wicked, nor stands in the way of sinners, nor sits in the seat of scoffers; but his delight is in the law of the LORD, and on his law he meditates day and night. He is like a tree planted by streams of water that yields its fruit in its season, and its leaf does not wither.

—PSALM 1:1-3

You, O LORD, are a shield about me, my glory, and the lifter of my head.

—PSALM 3:3

In peace I will both lie down and sleep; for you alone, O LORD, make me dwell in safety.

—PSALM 4:8

The LORD is my light and my salvation; whom shall I fear? The LORD is the stronghold of my life; of whom shall I be afraid?

—PSALM 27:1

The LORD is my strength and my shield; in him my heart trusts, and I am helped; my heart exults, and with my song I give thanks to him.

—PSALM 28:7

O LORD my God, I cried to you for help, and you have healed me.

—PSALM 30:2

I sought the LORD, and he answered me and delivered me from all my fears.

—PSALM 34:4

I waited patiently for the LORD; he inclined to me and heard my cry. He drew me up from the pit of destruction, out of the miry bog, and set my feet upon a rock, making my steps secure. He put a new song in my mouth, a song of praise to our God. Many will see and fear, and put their trust in the LORD.

—PSALM 40:1-3

God is our refuge and strength, a very present help in trouble.

—PSALM 46:1

For you, O LORD, are my hope.

—PSALM 71:5

He who dwells in the shelter of the Most High will abide in the shadow of the Almighty. I will say to the LORD, "My refuge and my fortress, my God, in whom I trust."

—PSALM 91:1-2

Because he holds fast to me in love, I will deliver him; I will protect him, because he knows my name. When he calls to me, I will answer him; I will be with him in trouble; I will rescue him and honor him. With long life I will satisfy him and show him my salvation.

—PSALM 91:14-16

Bless the LORD, O my soul, and forget not all his benefits, who forgives all your iniquity, who heals all your diseases, who redeems your life from the pit, who crowns you with steadfast love and mercy, who satisfies you with good so that your youth is renewed like the eagle's.

—PSALM 103:2-5

He sent out his word and healed them.

—PSALM 107:20

Your word is a lamp to my feet and a light to my path.

—PSALM 119:105

The LORD is your keeper; the LORD is your shade at your right hand. The sun shall not strike you by day, nor the moon by night. The LORD shall preserve you from all evil; He shall preserve your soul. The LORD shall preserve your going out and your coming in from this time forth, and even forevermore.

—PSALM 121, NKJV

Those who trust in the LORD are like Mount Zion, which cannot be moved, but abides forever.

—PSALM 125:1

O LORD, you have searched me and known me! You know when I sit down and when I rise up; you discern my thoughts from afar. You search out my path and my lying down and are acquainted with all my ways. Even before a word is on my tongue, behold, O LORD, you know it altogether. You hem me in, behind and before, and lay your hand upon me. Such knowledge is too wonderful for me; it is high; I cannot attain it.

Where shall I go from your Spirit? Or where shall I flee from your presence? If I ascend to heaven, you are there! If I make my bed in Sheol, you are there! If I take the wings of the morning and dwell in the uttermost parts of the sea, even there your hand shall lead me, and your right hand shall hold me. If I say, "Surely the darkness shall cover me, and the light about me be night," even the darkness is not dark to you; the night is bright as the day, for darkness is as light with you. For you formed my inward parts; you knitted me together in my mother's womb. I praise you, for I am fearfully and wonderfully made. Wonderful are your works; my soul knows it very well. My frame was not hidden from you, when I was being made in secret, intricately woven in the depths of the earth. Your eyes saw my unformed substance; in your book were written, every one of them, the days that were formed for me, when as yet there was none of them. How precious to me are your thoughts, O God! How vast is the sum of them! If I would count them, they are more than the sand. I awake, and I am still with you.

—PSALM 139:1-18

The eyes of all wait for You [looking, watching, and expecting] and You give them their food in due season. You open Your hand and satisfy every living thing with favor.

—PSALM 145:15-16, AMPC

He heals the brokenhearted and binds up their wounds.

—PSALM 147:3

Trust in the LORD with all your heart, and do not lean on your own understanding. In all your ways acknowledge him, and he will make straight your paths.

—PROVERBS 3:5-6

The LORD will be your confidence.

—PROVERBS 3:26

The name of the LORD is a strong tower; the righteous man runs into it and is safe.

—PROVERBS 18:10

Behold, you are beautiful, my love.

—SONG OF SOLOMON 1:16

Behold, God is my salvation; I will trust, and will not be afraid; for the LORD GOD is my strength and my song, and he has become my salvation.

—ISAIAH 12:2

You keep him in perfect peace whose mind is stayed on you, because he trusts in you. Trust in the LORD forever, for the LORD GOD is an everlasting rock.

—ISAIAH 26:3-4

And your ears shall hear a word behind you, saying, "This is the way, walk in it," when you turn to the right or when you turn to the left.

—ISAIAH 30:21

They who wait for the LORD shall renew their strength; they shall mount up with wings like eagles; they shall run and not be weary; they shall walk and not faint.

—ISAIAH 40:31

Remember not the former things, nor consider the things of

old. Behold, I am doing a new thing; now it springs forth, do you not perceive it? I will make a way in the wilderness and rivers in the desert.

—ISAIAH 43:18-19

But he was pierced for our transgressions; he was crushed for our iniquities; upon him was the chastisement that brought us peace, and with his wounds we are healed.

—ISAIAH 53:5

"The Spirit of the LORD God is upon Me, because the LORD has anointed Me to preach good tidings to the poor; He has sent Me to heal the brokenhearted, to proclaim liberty to the captives, and the opening of the prison to those who are bound; to proclaim the acceptable year of the LORD, and the day of vengeance of our God; to comfort all who mourn, to console those who mourn in Zion, to give them beauty for ashes, the oil of joy for mourning, the garment of praise for the spirit of heaviness; that they may be called trees of righteousness, the planting of the LORD, that He may be glorified."...But you shall be named the priests of the LORD, they shall call you the servants of our God.... Instead of your shame you shall have double honor, and instead of confusion they shall rejoice in their portion. Therefore in their land they shall possess double; everlasting joy shall be theirs.

—ISAIAH 61:1-3, 6-7, NKJV

Blessed is the man who trusts in the LORD, and whose hope is the LORD.

—JEREMIAH 17:7, NKJV

For I know the thoughts that I think toward you, says the LORD, thoughts of peace and not of evil, to give you a future and a hope. Then you will call upon Me and go and pray to Me, and I will listen to you. And you will seek Me and find Me, when you search for Me with all your heart.

—JEREMIAH 29:11-13, NKJV

I will sprinkle clean water on you, and you shall be clean.... And I will give you a new heart, and a new spirit I will put within you. And I will remove the heart of stone from your flesh and give you a heart of flesh. And I will put my Spirit within you, and cause you to walk in my statutes.

—EZEKIEL 36:25-27

Not by might, nor by power, but by my Spirit, says the LORD of hosts.

—ZECHARIAH 4:6

The Sun of Righteousness shall arise with healing in His wings.

—MALACHI 4:2

Look at the birds of the air: they neither sow nor reap nor gather into barns, and yet your heavenly Father feeds them. Are you not of more value than they?

—MATTHEW 6:26

But seek first the kingdom of God and his righteousness, and all these things will be added to you.

—MATTHEW 6:33

Come to me, all who labor and are heavy laden, and I will give you rest. Take my yoke upon you, and learn from me, for I am gentle and lowly in heart, and you will find rest for your souls. For my yoke is easy, and my burden is light.

—MATTHEW 11:28-30

For nothing will be impossible with God.

—LUKE 1:37

In the beginning was the Word, and the Word was with God, and the Word was God. He was in the beginning with God. All things were made through him, and without him was not any thing made that was made. In him was life, and the life was the light of men. The light shines in the darkness, and the darkness has not overcome it.

—JOHN 1:1-5

If you abide in My word, you are My disciples indeed. And you shall know the truth, and the truth shall make you free.

—JOHN 8:31-32, NKJV

I came that they may have life and have it abundantly.

—JOHN 10:10

I have overcome the world.

—JOHN 16:33, NIV

We have peace with God through our Lord Jesus Christ.... And not only this, but we also celebrate in our tribulations, knowing that tribulation brings about perseverance; and perseverance, proven character; and proven character, hope; and hope does not disappoint, because the love of God has been poured out within our hearts through the Holy Spirit who was given to us.

—ROMANS 5:1-5, NASB

There is therefore now no condemnation for those who are in Christ Jesus.

—ROMANS 8:1

And we know that for those who love God all things work together for good, for those who are called according to his purpose.

—ROMANS 8:28

In all these things we are more than conquerors through him who loved us.

—ROMANS 8:37

All the promises of God in Him are Yes, and in Him Amen, to the glory of God through us.

—2 CORINTHIANS 1:20, NKJV

Now thanks be to God who always leads us in triumph in Christ, and through us diffuses the fragrance of His knowledge in every place.

—2 CORINTHIANS 2:14

Since we have such a hope, we are very bold.

—2 CORINTHIANS 3:12

Therefore, if anyone is in Christ, he is a new creation; old things have passed away; behold, all things have become new.

—2 CORINTHIANS 5:17, NKJV

For the sake of Christ, then, I am content with weaknesses, insults, hardships, persecutions, and calamities. For when I am weak, then I am strong.

—2 CORINTHIANS 12:10

I have been crucified with Christ. It is no longer I who live, but Christ who lives in me. And the life I now live in the flesh I live by faith in the Son of God, who loved me and gave himself for me.

—GALATIANS 2:20

For freedom Christ has set us free.

—GALATIANS 5:1

But the fruit of the Spirit is love, joy, peace, patience, kindness, goodness, faithfulness, gentleness, self-control; against such things there is no law.

—GALATIANS 5:22-23

Those who belong to Christ Jesus have nailed the passions and desires of their sinful nature to his cross and crucified them there. Since we are living by the Spirit, let us follow the Spirit's leading in every part of our lives.

—GALATIANS 5:24-25, NLT

For we are his workmanship, created in Christ Jesus for good works, which God prepared beforehand, that we should walk in them.

—EPHESIANS 2:10

For this reason I bow my knees before the Father, from whom every family in heaven and on earth is named, that according to the riches of his glory he may grant you to be strengthened with power through his Spirit in your inner being, so that Christ may dwell in your hearts through faith—that you, being rooted and grounded in love, may have strength to comprehend with all the saints what is the breadth and length and height and depth, and to know the love of Christ that surpasses knowledge, that you may be filled with all the fullness of God.

—EPHESIANS 3:14-19

Now to him who is able to do far more abundantly than all that we ask or think, according to the power at work within us, to him be glory in the church and in Christ Jesus throughout all generations, forever and ever. Amen.

—EPHESIANS 3:20-21

...being confident of this, that he who began a good work in you will carry it on to completion until the day of Christ Jesus.

—PHILIPPIANS 1:6, NIV

I want you to know, brothers, that what has happened to me has really served to advance the gospel.

—PHILIPPIANS 1:12

God has not given us a spirit of fear, but of power and of love and of a sound mind.

2 TIMOTHY 1:7, NKJV

For the grace of God has been revealed, bringing salvation to all people. And we are instructed to turn from godless living and sinful pleasures. We should live in this evil world with wisdom, righteousness, and devotion to God, while we look forward with hope to that wonderful day when the glory of our great God and Savior, Jesus Christ, will be revealed. He gave his life to free us from every kind of sin, to cleanse us, and to make us his very own people, totally committed to doing good deeds.

—TITUS 2:11-14, NLT

For the word of God is living and active, sharper than any two-edged sword, piercing to the division of soul and of spirit, of joints and of marrow, and discerning the thoughts and intentions of the heart.

—HEBREWS 4:12

Let us hold fast the confession of our hope without wavering, for he who promised is faithful.

—HEBREWS 10:23

I will never leave you nor forsake you.

—HEBREWS 13:5

So we can confidently say, "The Lord is my helper; I will not fear."

—HEBREWS 13:6

Consider it pure joy, my brothers and sisters, whenever you face trials of many kinds, because you know that the testing of your faith produces perseverance. Let perseverance finish its work so that you may be mature and complete, not lacking anything.

—JAMES 1:2-4, NIV

As you come to him, a living stone rejected by men but in the sight of God chosen and precious, you yourselves like living stones are being built up as a spiritual house, to be a holy priesthood, to offer spiritual sacrifices acceptable to God through Jesus Christ.

—1 PETER 2:4-5

His divine power has granted to us all things that pertain to life and godliness, through the knowledge of him who called us to his own glory and excellence, by which he has granted to us his precious and very great promises.

—2 PETER 1:3-5

For everyone who has been born of God overcomes the world. And this is the victory that has overcome the world—our faith.

—1 JOHN 5:4

References

Chapter 5

1 Joyce Meyer Ministries, "ROBOT: What About Me? | Joyce Meyer," YouTube, January 15, 2015, https://www.youtube.com/watch?v=44yN5adYRaY.

2 Facing the Giants, dir. Alex Kendrick, Sherwood Pictures, 2006, https://www.youtube.com/watch?v=WAxwS8KyMQQ.

Chapter 6

1 Vibeke Lohne and Elisabeth Severinsson, "The power of hope: patients' experiences of hope a year after acute spinal cord injury," Journal of Clinical Nursing 15, no. 3 (March 2006): 315-323, https://doi.org/10.1111/j.1365- 2702.2006.01301.x; Anthony Scioli et al., "A Prospective Study of Hope, Optimism, and Health," Psychological Reports 81, no. 3 (1997), 723-733, https://doi.org/10.2466%2Fpr0.1997.81.3.723; Liz Day et al., "Hope uniquely predicts objective academic achievement above intelligence, personality, and previous academic achievement," Journal of Research in Personality 44, no.4 (August 2010): 550-553, https://doi.

org/10.1016/j.jrp.2010.05.009; Emma Pleeging, Martijn Burger, and Job van Exel, "The Relations between Hope and Subjective Well-Being: a Literature Overview and Empirical Analysis," Applied Research in Quality of Life 16 (2021): 1019–1041, https://doi.org/10.1007/s11482-019-09802-4.

2 Merriam-Webster, s.v. "hope," accessed October 12, 2021, https://www.merriam-webster.com/dictionary/hope.

3 Merriam-Webster, s.v. "hope."

4 Blue Letter Bible, s.v. "mibtāh," accessed October 12, 2021, https://www.blueletterbible.org/lexicon/h4009/kjv/wlc/0-1/.   5 Blue Letter Bible, s.v. "bātah," accessed October 12, 2021, https://www.blueletterbible.org/lexicon/h982/kjv/wlc/0-1/.

Chapter 7

1 Blue Letter Bible, s.v. "kānāp," accessed October 15, 2021, https://www.blueletterbible.org/lexicon/h3671/kjv/wlc/0-1/.

Chapter 8

1 Joyce Meyer, Battlefield of the Mind (New York: FaithWords, 2008), chapter 6, https://www.google.com/books/edition/Battlefield_of_the_Mind/8kl2TDV9kmoC?hl=en&gbpv=0.

2 Blue Letter Bible, s.v. "qāvâ," accessed October 18, 2021, https://www.blueletterbible.org/lexicon/h6960/kjv/wlc/0-1/.

3 Blue Letter Bible, s.v. "mᵊnaššê," accessed October 22, 2021, https://www.blueletterbible.org/lexicon/h4519/kjv/wlc/0-1/.   4 Blue Letter Bible, s.v. "ephrayim," accessed October 22, 2021,

https://www.blueletterbible.org/lexicon/h669/kjv/wlc/0-1/.

Chapter 9

1 Merriam-Webster, s.v. "perspective," accessed October 23, 2021, https://www.merriam- webster.com/dictionary/perspective.

2 Joni Eareckson Tada, Infinite Hope (Carol Stream, IL: Tyndale House, 2018), vii, https://www.amazon.com/Infinite-Hope-Midst-Struggles/dp/1496432231.

3 Blue Letter Bible, s.v. "kritikos," accessed October 24, 2021, https://www.blueletterbible.org/lexicon/g2924/kjv/tr/0-1/.

4 Merriam-Webster, s.v. "promise," accessed October 24, 2021, https://www.merriam- webster.com/dictionary/promise.

5 Blue Letter Bible, s.v. "epangelia," accessed October 24, 2021, https://www.blueletterbible.org/lexicon/g1860/kjv/tr/0-1/.

Chapter 10

1 Blue Letter Bible, s.v. "metamorphoō," October 30, 2021, https://www.blueletterbible.org/lexicon/g3339/kjv/tr/0-1/.

2 Blue Letter Bible, s.v. "hāzaq," accessed November 2, 2021, https://www.blueletterbible.org/lexicon/h2388/kjv/wlc/0-1/.

3 Blue Letter Bible, s.v. "hāzaq."

Chapter 11

1 Attributed to Vivian Greene.

2 Blue Letter Bible, s.v. "chorēgeō," accessed December 5, 2021, https://www.blueletterbible.org/lexicon/g5524/kjv/tr/0-1/.

3 Blue Letter Bible, s.v. "'ešer," accessed December 5, 2021, https://www.blueletterbible.org/lexicon/h835/kjv/wlc/0-1/.

Made in United States
Orlando, FL
09 November 2024

53659029R00104